CREATE THE
Love
OF YOUR LIFE

CREATE THE *Love* OF YOUR LIFE

Susan Scott

ZEBRA BOOKS
KENSINGTON PUBLISHING CORP.

ZEBRA BOOKS are published by

Kensington Publishing Corp.
475 Park Avenue South
New York, NY 10016

ISBN 0-8217-4180-2
Library of Congress Catalog Number: 93-077357

First Printing: June, 1993
Printed in the United States of America

This book is dedicated
    To all those who truly desire love and relationships of the
        highest nature
    To all those wanting to be the best they can be
    To learning and growing and enjoying the process
    To Christophe Stickel for being my loving soulmate
    To Thelma and Samuel Horowitz for being such loving parents
    To my loving friends and teachers
    To myself for staying on my own special journey
    To all the love this universe can hold

Contents

Introduction

Many of you today find it difficult to attain a fulfilling, intimate relationship. And those of you who are already in a relationship find it difficult to achieve the level of fulfillment necessary for personal satisfaction.

I believe that each of you has a "dream relationship" in your heart, a relationship that is what you want and need that will facilitate your growing both separately and together with your partner. If you have any other kind of relationship besides what you really want . . . you will not be happy. In *Create the Love of Your Life,* I will teach you how to successfully create your ideal relationship. No one ever has to settle for less than what they want in any relationship they create.

To create change in your relationships, you must do some things differently. Change and taking new risks is essential!

Why is a good relationship so difficult to achieve? Because often we are with the wrong person trying to make him or her become the right person. Every one of us has different expectations and needs and we can flounder for years in an unsatisfactory relationship unable to achieve what we desire. Also, most people go out looking for love, but searching is a big job. When we are looking and feeling even slightly needy, we will usually attract others who are needy, too. When you look you usually do not find.

And that's what this book is all about. Its premise is that each individual is responsible for the relationships he or she forms. And that anyone can create or have a good, fulfilling, committed relationship if that individual is willing to work toward it.

Personal History

My own path to writing this book began many years ago, when I walked away from both a marriage where "something was missing" and a thriving plastics business that my husband and I created. I started to question my life and dreams in ways I never had before. I left with empty pockets and my two-year-old son. I embarked on a new journey, certain that success was not based on monetary gains alone. I call this journey "my path to wisdom."

It was a journey sometimes filled with painful growth on deep inner levels. My determination to find the missing relationship pieces developed into a strong drive. In those days, I never knew where the path would actually lead.

Others looking in could have thought I was down on my luck. But my life wasn't over, it was just beginning. My "anything can happen" attitude turned tragedy into an adventure.

I was alone and isolated. My only resource was myself. Just by chance, I attended the Single Parent Support Group at the San Francisco Jewish Community Center. The minute I walked in the door I ceased to be alone. Together, members of the group shared their thoughts. No one had real answers to the questions we faced as we looked toward our futures and the futures of our children.

Often guest speakers would lead the discussions. When I was asked to lead a discussion, I was frightened because I had never done any public speaking before. I had been a bookkeeper for the last ten years.

But I accepted the challenge and chose as a topic, "The Positive Aspects of Being a Single Parent." At that point I couldn't think of even *one*. As I researched the program, I began to realize how much you can help yourself as you give to others. I intended for the attendees to walk away feeling positive and filled with new hopes and ideas. The program that evening turned many of us around.

When I got up in front of that group, it felt like I had been leading groups my whole life. I discovered, out of my personal tragedy, "my meant to be." I ended up leading the Single Parent Support Group for the next three and a half years. During that time over one thousand people attended.

Members of the group always wanted to know how to be more successful in their next relationship. I wanted to know, too, so I created many workshops based on the relationship issues that came up.

My research for the next eight years focused mainly on creating successful relationships and led me to become a relationship counselor. During that time I helped many others turn both personal and professional losses into wins.

The Love of Your Life Workshop was created in 1982 out of my vision to help people create love in powerful ways. I did this to put the missing pieces together for myself as much as I did to help others. As a result, I am happily remarried to my ideal partner.

This book is based on all of the positive results participants have achieved through the workshop.

About This Book

My purpose for writing this book is to have as many of you as possible learn how to create what you want and need both in your relationship with yourself and in your relationships with others. Whether you are alone or currently with a partner, this book will assist you in achieving the highest level of a relationship possible. It is dedicated to the principle that anything is attainable when you have prepared yourself for the relationship you really want. With the right person in your life you will be happier, healthier, more productive, more prosperous, and more creative. You will grow more as an individual, and learn how to grow together as a couple with your partner. You will know inner peace and joy in new ways. Everyone and everything moves forward out of healthy love and healthy relationships.

The book is divided into three parts.

In Part I, Beginning, you will begin to get a clear perspective on your present relationship circumstance and then begin to clarify what you ideally want. You will begin to understand the importance of the lessons that can be learned in your relationships and how to relate them to your present and future relationship success.

In Part II, Creating, you will decide exactly what you need in the various areas of relationship such as intimacy, trust, communication, and respect, and how to bring those issues into alignment with who you are and what your goals are. You will discover what obstacles you place in the way of a satisfying relationship and how to remove or transform them. You will find out how to make changes easily. You will learn to increase your confidence and personal power, begin to integrate the spiritual and practical dimensions of a relationship and learn exactly how to "create" the Love of Your Life.

In Part III, Succeeding, you will learn to prepare for your ideal relationship by taking a personal inventory of the qualities you possess that will attract a relationship or help you to bond more deeply with the partner you are already with. You will get ready for a new and more rewarding relationship challenge. Next, you will find out how to keep a relationship alive, growing and successful.

Reading and implementing the information in this book will be comparable to attending Relationship School—its pages are the instructions needed to make the love you deserve obtainable. And may you find and enjoy all the love, inner peace, and joy you are meant to have.

SECTION I

BEGINNING

Chapter One

Anything is Possible in a Relationship

Nothing is impossible to a willing heart.
—John Heywood

Each person reading this book will be going through the same process, but the results will be different for everyone. Everyone is in a different place and on a different relationship level.

It doesn't matter where you are now, single or married, just know that you will benefit from this new road you are about to take. How much you put into the process of change will determine your results. You can expect some change to occur from reading and working with this book. But just reading the words alone will not accomplish your relationship goals.

You will not obtain everything you want in a relationship no matter what you do. You can get most of what you want, though. I've seen many individuals come close. But, like everything else, there will always be new challenges to work on.

As you go through the chapters, many pieces of the puzzle will begin to fit together. You will see how all the different relationship issues are connected to each other. It is like a car engine. If you have great spark plugs and a good carburetor, but are missing a valve, the car won't run. If you have great sex and romance but are missing intimacy or communication, the relationship will run at about half speed.

Whether you are alone now, or in a relationship, you will always be undergoing a growth process. We grow faster in relationships because more issues surface to work on.

As you continue growing and changing your relationships will change. In addition, other people will begin to respond to you differently because you will be different.

As you complete this process here are some of the results you can achieve:

- You will clarify what kind of relationship you want.
- You will clarify what your needs are.
- You will discover what obstacles are in the way of your relationship dreams.
- You will learn how to make the needed changes.
- You will learn the secrets of keeping relationships alive and growing.
- You will achieve a deeper understanding of yourself and others.
- You will increase your confidence and personal power.
- You will achieve a new perspective on your past, present, and future relationships.
- You will learn how to integrate the spiritual and practical dimensions of a relationship.
- You will learn what it takes to create the love of your life.

We have had an extremely high success rate with the participants in The Love of Your Life Workshops. Single people have created brand new intimate partners. And couples and married people have created much stronger bonding as they realign themselves and the relationship.

Let me give you some examples.

One of our couples, Rita, a legal secretary and Tom, an accountant, had been living together for four years, unable to commit to each other. They were stuck and needed to make changes. Only Rita attended the workshop. She called me the following day to say they became engaged. After she understood the process, and shared it with Tom, they had been able to move to the next place.

Another couple, Margaret and Richie, who had been going together for two years, were extremely unhappy with the way their relationship was going. He had an unstable future in the music business. She had two small children and needed a secure life-style. Together they were miserable, but they couldn't leave each other. After attending the workshop they saw clearly that they must take separate paths to get what they wanted. It was easier for them to separate and create new partners, than to try to keep a relationship together that was going in two directions.

Both partners in another relationship were prosperous, good looking, smart, and successful. Vickie and Steve were bright professional business people and made a tremendous couple. I always enjoyed their lively energy. Unfortunately, they had a long history of being unable to trust prior intimate partners and each other. As a result, they couldn't get the full benefit of their relationship. After attending the workshop, they began to work on trusting. The last I heard they had bought a house together.

Another participant was a successful author of eight books. He had dated many women over a nine-year period, had been nonmonogamous, but was still looking for "the right one." He flew in for the workshop from another state. After going through the Intimate Process, he finally understood what he wanted. Within a few months he created his ideal woman, and shortly after that they moved in together. This was his first commitment in nine years.

Still another couple, Tina and Fred, had been married nine years and were now on the brink of divorce after couples counseling and a lot of hard work. They had many hopes and dreams about their marriage and new career paths. After attending the workshop, they realized they had everything they needed with each other, they just weren't putting the parts together in the right way. Over the next few months they created a brand new union and are now happier than ever before. They also successfully changed their professions.

The success stories go on and on. But there is one special case I want to share. When I first met my client, Raymond, I was sure he didn't have much of a chance. I rarely felt that way about anyone. Raymond was in his middle forties and was totally blind where women were concerned. He was unskilled in connecting with people and just couldn't make a relationship work. I certainly wouldn't have bet money on him, yet Raymond wanted to get married and have a child.

He came for several private sessions before attending the workshop. He learned from every lesson, and within a short time I received a wedding announcement. A year later he called to tell me they had a baby son. Raymond is a big inspiration for me. He convinced me that anything is possible in a relationship.

I didn't make it happen for Raymond or for any of the others. They all turned their lives around themselves in different ways. And it has been as exciting for me to watch as it was to experience the process of creation for myself.

Where Are You Now?

Stop for a moment now and take stock of what kind of relationship exists in your life. Does what you have match up to what you want? How close does it come to matching? The answer to these questions are an indication of how much work you have ahead of you.

Imagine for a moment that you have read this book, took all the needed steps to create the wanted results, and you have "created" your ideal relationship. How does that make you feel? Is your body relaxed or filled with anxiety? Do you feel proud or scared when you imagine having the relationship you always wanted?

Being willing to "create" your ideal relationship also means that you will do whatever it takes. You must go beyond your fears, open your heart, be vulnerable and take new risks. You will have to make changes and let go of old ways and patterns. Are you willing to do that?

I've come across some individuals who aren't in touch with even the desire to have a relationship. At a large singles group, I met a woman who boasted that she didn't need anyone. She was proud that the phone didn't ring and that she spent her time alone. I imagined her living in a fortress with walls around it. When I asked how long she had been coming to the singles group, she replied, "Every Monday night for the past eight years."

Before we go any further, I want you to take an attitude check. Do you feel positive that you can create the relationship you want? Are you willing to work at your lessons in-between? How much do you really want to go on this new journey?

Henry Ford said, "People who think they can and people who think they can't are both right!"

Getting Started

I suggest you read Sections I, II, and III in sequence for the best results. In Section II you do not have to read each chapter in sequence but it is important that you do complete Chapters 4 thru 15 before doing The Intimate Process in Chapter 16. All of the information prior to Chapter 16 prepares you for the Intimate Process, in which you will "create" the relationship you really want. This process is designed to bring to you a certain level of clarity and understanding about each of the different aspects of relationship needed before your relationship construction begins. Also, you will become more aware of how each issue is connected to the other issues in relationships.

Of course, you have to be willing to have your ideal relationship in order to create it. How you use this information will indicate how willing you are to take that next step. The more work, time, and energy you put into this process, the more you will get out of it.

I recommend that couples process all information and do all of the exercises individually first and then share and compare your new ideas and plans with each other. Do the exercises with your mate only after you have implemented them alone first.

There is no set way a relationship is suppose to look. There are no rules in relationships, period. The possibilities of what relationships can be are limitless. Anything is possible when you are the one creating them.

You are the only one who can set the guidelines of what works for you. You are learning how to create what you want. You don't want to go by anyone else's rules, but know that you can relearn anything you need to about human relations. And you can start over at any given moment.

From now on, consider this book your new beginning.

Chapter Two

What is an Ideal Relationship?

Success is getting what you want. Happiness is wanting what you get.

—Anonymous

Ideal, in a relationship, means having what you want and need. Let's say, for instance, as a man, you want a devoted and affectionate partner who will help you achieve your goals in life. When you find this person, you have achieved this ideal. As a woman, you may want a man who shares the workload at home and gives you plenty of time to develop your own career. Or you may want someone who is taller than you are and is exceptionally handsome.

In my own case, I am a busy person with a life dedicated to my work. To achieve my ideal . . . and contentment, I knew I had to be with a mate who had the same interest in his work as I did, and who was understanding and undemanding. To achieve your ideal, you need to do what I did . . . to identify the kind of a mate, or relationship that comfortably fits your way of life.

While you will be working with this book alone, it is intended for both singles and couples. If you are part of a couple or married, approach the issues that are presented as an individual person and then apply them to your own existing relationship. I find that as I continue to grow and move forward, my marriage expands in many positive ways.

The Problem of Settling

Unfortunately in this search for an ideal relationship, many people settle for something short of what they really want. My own belief is that when you do this, it never really works. If you do not have what you want and need in a relationship, you will ultimately be unhappy. You will also feel "off" and out of balance with yourself.

When you settle for a so-so relationship, you often try to make the other person into what you want them to be rather than letting them be themselves. One of my workshop participants, Clara, is a clinical psychologist who earns over a hundred thousand dollars a year. She is well regarded in her field and speaks to groups nationwide. Clara's problem is that she desperately wants a relationship, no matter what she has to settle for. So far, I have seen her go through several partners. All of them have jobs far inferior to hers, all have borrowed money from her, and all but one has cheated on her during the relationship. Clara herself has an extremely outgoing personality, but the men she dates are the dullest I have ever met. Most can't carry on a conversation.

Clara always pretends she enjoys her partner's company but she confided to me that every one of them has bored her to death. Unfortunately, she wants a relationship so desperately she's willing to settle for almost anything. Eventually, in every relationship, her energy wears down and she finally has to stop pretending that her present man is the right one for her, or that she is really happy. Clara, in her desperation, gives off phony energy. As a result, she keeps attracting phony relationships. This keeps her in a self-repeating cycle.

In addition to desperately needing a relationship, I have

discovered that people also settle for money, prestige, "someone to love me," "someone to take care of me," "someone to save me," good looks, good sex, security, companionship, having children, making parents happy, settling down because the time is right, and more.

As one of my clients, Mary Lou, a bank teller, told me, "I don't really love my boyfriend Gerald, in fact I don't even like being around him. But he's vice president of his company, drives an expensive car, and belongs to the right clubs. As a result all my friends envy me. Sometimes, however, I have a hard time convincing myself it's worth it."

Another client, thirty-nine-year-old Roger, explained that he had never been very good with women and because of this, he had never gone out with a woman he considered good looking. Then he met Janet, the most beautiful woman he had ever seen. Much to his amazement she returned his attention. She, however, continuously flirted with other men, was unfaithful several times, and threw temper tantrums when he arrived late. After telling me this, he said, "I can't stand to break up with her . . . she's so beautiful. I don't want to lose her, but I don't like being around her either."

And one final example. Geraldine, a twenty-nine-year-old interesting and bright attorney, recently married an unemployed man she met on vacation in the Caribbean. "I have a great career going," she told me, "but time is running out. All my girlfriends are married and I want and need children. When Ron asked me to marry him I jumped at the chance. It's not an ideal relationship, but I'll settle for this because I have this overwhelming feeling that I shouldn't wait."

I always feel sad when I hear stories like this. The reason is that I know no one ever has to settle for less than they want and need.

An additional problem related to settling is closing your eyes to the other person's faults. Some people want the relationship to work so badly that they either ignore what the other person is really like, or lie to themselves about his or her bad habits. One example is the case of one of my female clients, Judy, a creative fashion designer. Her boyfriend of two and a half months, Albert, an antique dealer, kept trying to get her to lend him a large chunk of her savings. We all told her that he only wanted money, but she wouldn't listen. Finally she gave him the ten thousand dollars he kept asking for. Two weeks later, he moved to another town with an old girlfriend. That was a tough experience for Judy, but it taught her the lesson she needed to learn before she could give herself permission to create the relationship she really wanted and deserved.

Unfortunately, I often see people hiding the facts about others. If you will open your eyes, you can nearly always tell when something is wrong. I instruct my clients to keep their senses tuned through touch, taste, smell, and sight. There are always clues. The partner may act nervous, he or she may continually avoid looking into your eyes, or say something which is later proved untrue.

Bob, a client of mine, found that his girlfriend Laura tended to fidget and rub her hands whenever he talked about going out with her on Wednesday night. Later it turned out that Laura had been having an affair with a married man for a number of years and the only night they could get together was Wednesday. She neglected to tell Bob about it. At first, Bob tried to ignore the clues, but it became obvious something was wrong. And when he confronted her, she admitted the truth.

I also sometimes find, that when the other person is cheating, they overcompensate and become especially thoughtful. They will bring flowers or candy when the occasion doesn't warrant or insist on doing something they wouldn't ordinarily do. Most people are sincere and honest, but I find it pays to go into every relationship with your eyes wide open. In addition I feel you should be prepared to cut off the relationship if you aren't getting what you want. That doesn't mean you don't work with whatever problems you find. After all, relationships sometimes need to be nurtured. But once you decide that it is impossible to save, then you must be true to yourself.

I also want to warn you about waiting for someone to change to fit your needs. In most cases it never happens. One of my workshop participants, Doris, a thirty-year-old model, moved in with a man she felt was perfect for her in every way. He and Doris took frequent cruises, went to the theater together, and spent endless evenings in front of the fireplace, talking about everything from art to women's liberation. The problem was that Doris wanted a committed relationship, Stan didn't. She told herself that he would change in time. After almost five years, however, his desires remained the same and Doris had to admit that he would probably never be able to commit to her. If she ever expected a committed relationship, she decided, she simply had to find someone else.

What Do You Really Want?

In order to create what you do want, you must first clearly focus on what you sincerely need. Some of the positive things people in my workshops say they want in a relationship are fun, a positive attitude, warmth, reliability, power, openness, a sense of humor, poise, flexibility, uniqueness, neatness, caring, commitment, loving, sensuality, passion, sincerity, aliveness, self-knowledge, clarity, integrity, playfulness, an outgoing personality, energy, calmness, happiness, trustworthiness, consideration, a hard-working partner, tolerance, conscientiousness, romance, empowerment, confidence, physically fit, self-loving, compassionate, punctual, honest, nonjudgmental, a good communicator, kindness, and attractiveness. These are just a few to get you started. As you go through the learning chapters that follow, you will discover many more that are important to you.

What I want you to begin doing now, however, is to become

clear about your needs. Clarity means knowing what you have, what you don't have, and what you need. In order to see these things you *must* pay attention to the truth. Become an observer by stepping aside, neutralizing yourself, and looking at what is really happening from a detached place. This is sometimes difficult to do.

If you're already part of a couple you might discover that what you need and what you already have do not match. Since one premise of this book is that each individual is responsible for the relationships he or she forms, many changes can occur in your relationship or marriage just from your own process of change. Those changes can be attitudinal, emotional, spiritual, or physical. You may discover as you become clearer about your needs that you are absolutely with the right person for you but some different actions may need to be taken. Or you may discover the differences are just too great and splitting up is inevitable. Again, it is only out of telling the truth about what actually is, that you will create what you really want and need. It is also out of telling the truth that you can begin to heal the past and present.

It helps if you take a few minutes every day. Go to a quiet place, sit down, and go over what's happening. Try to see this from a distance, then ask yourself what is important (to you) in this situation, and what isn't.

One other thing I want to impress on you is that true happiness is being what you really are and having those things in your life that you really need. Clarity, I have discovered, helps put you on the track toward happiness.

I also want you to make sure that what you say you want, is what you really want. I often find, in my workshops, that some people simply can't put the two together.

Say What You Want

Once you have a general idea of your needs, I want you to make a statement about the kind of relationship you want. For example you might indicate *"I want a monogamous marriage,"* *"I want a live-in lover,"* *"I want a loving friendship."* You can verbalize it out loud, affirm it silently to yourself, or you can write it down. The more you say what you want, the more you are putting it out in the universe, and the more commitment you will feel toward yourself and your goals. Saying what you want is the first step toward overcoming fears of vulnerability.

Now list details to go along with your description. Be sure and save your list for use later in the book.

What we do in our The Love of Your Life workshops is to decide in great detail what each person wants out of a relationship, then we prepare for that relationship by matching our personality to the desired relationship. You've just taken the first step here. I want a best friend I can go to the deepest of the deep both sexually and mentally. ♥

Chapter Three

Basic Facts About Relationships

*Relationship is life, and this relationship is a
constant movement, a constant change.*
—J. Krisnamurti
You Are the World

My definition of a relationship is "how you want to be with
someone." It implies that you decide what you need and then
create it.

Frances Vaughn, psychologist, author of *The Inward Arc,*
has worked with many people on their death beds. When she
asked what mattered most to them in their lives, without excep-
tion, they said their relationships. It was the people they spent
time with, not their cars and condos!

Charles Garfield, author of *Peak Performance,* researched
the characteristics of high achievers and discovered that they all
have a happy family life that included a healthy relationship.

Now, let me show you how a relationship can be tailored to
your individual needs. I have a professional client named Elaine
who lives a hectic Monday to Friday life, putting in ten to fifteen
hours a day. During the week she often flies from city to city
handling difficult problems for her law firm.

On weekends, however, she likes to disappear into her California beach condo emerging only on Monday morning. "How
she wanted to be with someone," was to spend a quiet weekend

with another person listening to music, reading, walking on the beach, indulging her hobby of Cajun cooking.

At a seminar, she met a stressed-out executive who confided to her that he really needed someplace to escape on weekends and someone to share that escape with. And that's the kind of relationship they created. No matter where they are now, they fly into California on Friday night, spend the weekend together, and head out Monday morning.

Of course, there are many reasons to have a relationship. Some of these reasons involve long-term psychological needs, others have to do with a short-term need for companionship.

Long-term needs might include: to share life's experience and future with another . . . to work together to achieve common dreams and goals . . . to keep from spending old age alone . . . to have someone to trade ideas with . . . to satisfy the tension created by a ticking biological clock, and more.

Short-term companionship needs include: having someone to take a trip to Europe with, go hiking with on weekends, attend the opera with, and more.

One of my clients, Shari, came to one of my workshops to "create" a roommate. She needed to share her house with some-one to reduce expenses, yet that person had to be compatible since my client ran a computer service out of her home.

Her roommate must respect what she did, work somewhere else during the day, and remain quiet when at home. Within two weeks, Shari found a student who only studied at home.

Another young woman I know had a compelling need to discuss everything. Betsy was a stunning redhead who had very strong opinions about politics, religion, and the environment. She would go on and on about women's rights every chance she got, and sexual harassment was her favorite topic.

As a result, she had a basic need to create a relationship in which she could talk about her views on life, and in which she could vent her strong opinions anytime she wanted to. What she wanted was for someone to talk to her about her views and to be a good listener. Without this, life just wasn't worth living for her. Eventually, she did create this relationship, although I'm not sure it lasted.

Of course, despite all of these other reasons, love is probably always the basis for every deep relationship. Everyone has a deep-seated need to be loved by someone else and in return to give love. Without love, most people feel incomplete.

Some individuals might not realize this if they are out of touch with their feelings. In addition, sometimes men and women who have been hurt in a relationship, or who are extremely self-centered, will deny that they can ever be in love. After all, when they fall in love with someone else, they can't always keep full control in their own hands. The truth is that love is always needed to complete a deep relationship.

I sometimes see men who feel their basic needs include having a tall blonde on their arm to show off and impress business associates. I have also seen both men and women who feel the main reason for a relationship is to have sex.

I had one professional client who was obsessed with sex. Herb was about forty-five, a soft-spoken, kind, and gentle man. He frequently created relationships with women just for the purpose of having sex. None of his sexual relationships seldom lasted more than a few months. In one of my workshops, Herb met a woman who thought he was tremendous, but she had set her sights on a long-term committed relationship. When she realized that he wasn't interested in a deep commitment, she broke off the relationship immediately.

He quickly moved on to someone else, but couldn't seem to get her out of his mind. "I finally realized that I was in love with her," he told me, "and that this was the real reason for the relationship. I could have sex with a lot of women, but I seem to be capable of loving only a select few, or maybe even only one."

All reasons for having a relationship are valid, and you

should not try to fool yourself about your reasons. Always ask yourself what your *real* needs are in each relationship.

To discover this, just look within and ask yourself what you have been getting out of a current or past relationship.

Lessons

Our relationships affect everything we do. Every frustration or problem we have, whether it is our health, our work, our money is connected to our unresolved relationship issues.

I had one client, twenty-seven and attractive, who had a good job as an office manager for a real-estate firm. Sylvia adored her job. Her problem was she didn't trust her live-in boyfriend. Somehow, she was sure he was seeing someone else behind her back. This belief kept her from concentrating on her profession with the needed intensity. During one week she made several mistakes that cost the firm a seven-thousand-dollar deal. At the end of the week her boss let her go . . . a direct result of a relationship problem.

Life problems always seem to be connected with unresolved relationship issues. As we resolve each of these issues, we also seem to resolve the problems in the other areas of our lives.

In addition, it is important to see failed relationships not as failures, but as learning experiences. In general, relationships allow you to learn how you want to be treated, and what you must do to have someone else treat you that way.

For instance, emotionally unstable people upset you, so you need to learn that you don't want someone who doesn't deal with anger well. Or you have a busy schedule, and need to learn that you must have someone who is flexible. Or you get your feelings hurt easily and need to learn that you can't live with someone who is insensitive. You hate to be nagged at, so your lesson is to learn that you need someone who accepts you as you are.

Remember, if your relationships continually break up, you have not failed. It just means that you don't yet understand the lessons you need to learn.

It also means that same lesson will keep coming up until you get it right. If you give up because your relationships don't work out, you will miss out on your best growth experiences. If it is an ideal relationship, you will learn your lessons and keep growing. If you are growth oriented and unable to work it through, then the person may not be appropriate for you.

A young secretary named Ellen constantly worked to improve her life. She took night classes to upgrade her skills, joined Toastmasters and began to enhance her communication skills. Her male companion, however, wanted her home every evening, and demanded that she stop trying to make him look bad. Finally, he gave her an ultimatum: spend more time with him or get out. Ellen packed up and left that evening. The relationship, she concluded, was a mismatch. Her lesson was that she had to keep growing and developing her potential as much as possible.

When clients come for counseling after a breakup, I always ask them to look at what they learned from that relationship. Asking the simple question, "What are your positive lessons?" puts it in perspective. They can immediately see what they gained, not just what they lost. If they can list their positive lessons, they are really making progress. If they cannot find one positive lesson, they either have an ego problem that must be overcome, or they are temporarily paralyzed with fear.

One professional woman, a client of mine named Bethany, broke up with her partner, a prominent banker, after dating him for almost three years. "I was ready to settle down," she told me. "But he wanted more freedom than I gave him. I always tried to hold him too tightly. We always fought over how possessive I'd become."

He also had the habit of putting off tasks that were important to him and to me. I guess I thought I could change him."

"Okay," I said. "Now what lessons have you learned?"

"People are often in separate emotional places," she told me. "If one individual in a relationship is ready to settle down and the other isn't, it isn't going to work. Everyone needs their space. I need my space, I just have a hard time giving it to others.

"In addition I learned that you must accept someone for what they are, not try to change him or her."

Once you recognize what lessons you are working on, and you believe that you have learned them, then you go on to the next lesson.

There will always be lessons to be learned. You will never reach a point where you know everything. But the more ideal a relationship is, the higher level the issues and the lessons will be.

A deep passionate relationship, for instance, might bring out jealousy in you that you didn't know existed, or it may make you realize that you expect too much.

To see what issues you are working on, take a few minutes now to look at the relationships that are presently in your life. Your relationships are your mirrors, so ask yourself, what issues keep coming up? They tell you exactly who you are, where you are, and what you need to do. They will also affirm what you want and don't want in a relationship.

For instance, if you find yourself getting angry every time your mate contradicts you, that's an issue you're working on. Or, suppose you feel your partner isn't telling you the truth. Look within yourself. Maybe you lack confidence in yourself and because of it also lack confidence in everyone else.

It is also true that often, whatever bothers you about someone is exactly what you need to work on yourself. If you are working on trust, you will probably have someone in your life who you do not totally trust. You will be wondering where they really are on a Saturday night. If you are working on patience, you will probably have someone in your life who is much slower than you.

I'd like to also offer a piece of advice. When you are in an intimate relationship and your mate isn't getting his or her lesson, do not cross over into the role of counselor and attempt to point out the problems. This simply leads to trouble since they will react to you emotionally, not logically. If they need professional help, direct them to it, but never mix up your role.

We all work on our lessons at different speeds. Sometimes we will finish our lessons fast, and sometimes very slowly. In addition, your mate may be going through the same process at a totally different speed than you are.

You can't hurry the process, because sometimes you may have a number of lessons going on at the same time. In addition, one of your lessons may be to slow down . . . take things easy . . . and in that portion of your life, be a snail.

When you are working on more than one lesson at a time, it often shows up as multiple troubles in your life. Remember when everything that could go wrong, did at the very same time? Just as you found out that your boyfriend or girlfriend was sleeping with someone else, your job became jeopardized, your rent was raised, and your mother needed serious surgery.

It is amazing how we seem to create just what we need to work on. One of the rules of lessons is that you will attract to you what you need to learn. In addition, remember that no matter what is going on with anyone else, it is always *your* lesson.

Now let's take a closer look at the example above. It is easy to understand that the unfaithfulness of your boyfriend or girl-friend might be "your" lesson. You may be attracting people who simply lack character and can't be faithful. Or, you might be driving the other person into someone else's arms by your own actions. This is easy to accept. But what about your job? Your rent being raised? Your mother's surgery? Surely, they aren't *your* lessons. Of course they are. Perhaps the firm you work for has lost contracts and as a result laid you off. Is that your fault? Of course not. But the lesson to be learned is that this kind of thing happens. Be alert for it, and try to take action before you get caught. It's a lesson that can help you in the future.

The lesson of all the rest of these is that things happen, so you need to be emotionally prepared, or prepare in advance so you won't be taken by surprise. Some people encounter problems like this all the time. Their luck is constantly bad. Others always seem to do the right thing . . . all the time. The first type of person lets things happen to him or to her, the second has learned the lesson and stays alert so he or she can take action before a problem arises.

Marriage Today

The divorce rate is high today and keeps varying from one out of three to one out of two divorces per marriage. In the near future, it is expected to go even higher than this . . . but people keep remarrying.

What does this mean? We want more security and committed love than ever before, but many of us do not know how to make it last. Actually, most of the time people marry the wrong partner because they do not have the necessary skills to create the appropriate person for themselves nor the skills to keep a marriage growing and expanding.

Caroline, a young teacher, married right out of college because she thought it was the thing to do. Unfortunately, her new husband ignored her almost from the beginning. Often, he would come home late, watch television for a few hours, and go to bed without saying anything to her. Although she begged him to communicate more, he ignored her pleas. Within a few months, she realized she had made a terrible mistake and filed for divorce. The person she had selected was wrong for her and was destructive to both her happiness and potential for growth. The truth is that it is very difficult to grow and expand within a marriage when you are married to the wrong person.

Even if you really love the other person that love is never enough to keep any relationship together, married or not.

We need to learn the skills to create appropriate partners and also the skills to maintain, expand, and enhance those relationships. If both spouses want a marriage and are willing to work at the relationship, however, then there is a real good chance of success.

Pilot School

If you wanted to fly an airplane wouldn't you go to pilot school first? Yet, all of us want to have quality relationships without having gone to relationship school. Can you imagine learning to fly while in the air?

The truth is that you need to educate yourself in relationship basics, just as you would need to educate yourself about how to fly if you intended to fly an airplane. We make conscious decisions whether or not we are going to learn something. The more time and energy you put into relationship school, the more that will come back to you and affect you positively. This entire book, of course, can be considered relationship school. When you finish you will understand many of the elements needed to create and maintain the relationship you want. Just as you would if you were learning to fly, you need to take these lessons seriously and go over them as many times as you need to understand them clearly.

Types of Relationships

There is no standard or "normal" type of relationship today. When choosing the relationship you would like to have, make sure it fits your wants and needs and that it supports your purpose in life.

Listed below are some of the types of relationships you can create. Remember, what you want in a relationship right now may change to another type of relationship at another time. Here are the types to consider:

Friendship: A friend is someone you trust and care about. A friend is also someone with whom you can let down your hair and who trusts you enough to ask you for help.

Sexual: A purely sexual relationship is one used to satisfy sexual needs when you are afraid of intimacy. Often, a person who is looking primarily for a sexual relationship is not available on an emotional level.

Marriage—monogamous (exclusive): Monogamous marriage is self-explanatory. The advantage of a monogamous marriage is that the trust level is high, enough to build a future on.

Marriage—with other partners (open): Many people tried this type of relationship before the AIDS crisis. I have to admit that I have never seen one work, but they do fit some people's temporary needs.

Primary—monogamous: This is not a marriage, but a relationship where the partners are committed to each other. A primarily monogamous relationship can and usually does include both friendship and sex.

Primary—with other partners: The partners in this relationship are still shopping. They are usually unhappy and dissatisfied to some degree in the relationship and are constantly looking.

Multiple partners: These relationships can sometimes work if they are out in the open. However, they are usually unstable because your energy and attention becomes scattered.

Group marriage: Group marriage satisfies a number of needs, since it allows the partners to divide up the chores that occur in any marriage. You see very few of these around in today's climates.

Transitional/healing: These are typical of relationships that many of us go through. Our partner isn't someone we want to settle down with, but it can provide companionship, or a healing period after the breakup of a more serious relationship. This is also a relationship that helps rebuild self-confidence.

Levels of Relationships

We are all on levels of relationships ranging from beginning to advanced. Most people would like to have relationships with someone on an advanced level, but if you are on a beginning level, someone on an advanced level probably would not be interested in you. They have done a lot more work on themselves than you have and would become bored or drained.

Usually, we attract people to us who are close to the same level that we are on. When two people are on significantly different levels, one low (beginning) and one high (advanced) the low one brings the high one down.

For example, Marilyn, a social worker and a client I had known for years, knew how to communicate well with her partner, show patience, and offer support. Unfortunately, John demanded she stop talking to any other man and refused to listen to anything she had to say in her own defense. Marilyn had learned many of her lessons, and was ready for a strong committed relationship. John was still on level one, as far as relationship readiness was concerned. Within a few months John had so undermined Marilyn's confidence that she didn't feel capable of loving or even supporting anyone anymore.

If you are already part of a couple and have a strong commitment to your personal growth but your partner doesn't, you could run into a possible problem. This is an area where I feel it's important for both people to be on similar levels of evolvement. Otherwise, you could outgrow your partner, feel held back personally, or be unable to function well as a pair and in moving forward together.

A good example of this principle would be Margaret and Mike, a married couple of fifteen years. Margaret is a nurse and Mike a mechanic. They sought couples counseling to bring back some long lost sparkle into their marriage. After talking with them I discovered that Margaret had not allowed herself to progress in her career and in certain aspects of her personal development because she was fearful she would lose Mike if she became too powerful.

Margaret knew that if she had made some of those powerful changes in her life over the years, she would have outgrown Mike and have had to leave the marriage. Mike had never put any energy into developing his "full potential" and preferred staying the same, year after year.

You can certainly renew the sparkle within a marriage if that sparkle already exists. But you cannot expect to move forward to higher relationship levels as a couple when both partners are not progressing on your own personal issues.

For an exercise, answer these questions: What relationship level do you think you are on? If you already have a partner what level do you think he or she is on? Now ask your partner these same two questions. The answers could give each of you some new perspectives from which to proceed.

As you work to resolve the issues that come up and you both

continue to grow, you will move to higher levels. The higher the level you are on, the deeper the issues you will work on. If your relationship issues go unresolved, however, you will either stay on the same level or more likely move down to a lower level.

SECTION II

CREATING

Chapter Four

What is Love?

Life is the flower of which love is the honey.
—Victor Hugo

Although love means many different things to everyone, mostly having to do with feelings of affection and admiration for yourself or others, it is of course much more than that. To me love means joy. It is hard to think about love without thinking about how love feels. Some people say love feels magical, special, tingly, exciting. Others say they are more productive when in love. I've seen both men and women halt everything in their lives and focus on nothing else except their newly found love.

I'd like to ask you to stop now and ask yourself: How do I feel when I'm in love? Think about it for a little while. Is the feeling healing? Do you feel out of touch with the world? Do you have a super-awareness of what's happening around you? Or what? Being in touch with these feelings will heighten your creative process for it fills us with many positive feelings.

Remember how you felt when you first fell in love? You became filled with "love energy." When this happens, people who seemed unattainable to you before suddenly become interested in you. It seems like a lot of people are attracted to you when you are in love. But, of course, now you are unavailable!

Several years ago, I met a client for lunch who I hadn't seen for some time. I knew the minute Joyce walked in the restaurant that she was in love. She had a glow about her, and her eyes sparkled. Her conversation bubbled with energy, and as she talked, I could see that for her the future looked bright.

In the course of the conversation, she told me about her boyfriend, an executive in a local advertising agency, and how she felt about him. She also told me that since she had fallen in love, several men who had ignored her before had called her for dates. Joyce couldn't seem to understand why, but I could. Her "love energy" attracted love and positive attention.

Love is powerful energy that feeds our soul. We need it to survive and we need to give and receive it, but only in equal and balanced ways. Love is life. Author and psychologist Leo Buscaglia, defines love as the ultimate expression of the will to live!

Babies who are denied love have their growth and development seriously affected. Sometimes it even causes death.

You can be part of a couple or even married and still not feel love if you are unable to receive it or if your needs far exceed the love and affection that your partner makes available to you.

Wanting love has a lot to do with wanting attention. You don't always get love by giving love. You get love by being able to receive love.

Some psychologists say that many of us do everything we do in order to get love: how we dress, what we say, and how we act. For the most part, this is subconscious. But some people set out deliberately to try to make someone love them. And the truth is, that generally it doesn't work. You can't make someone love you because you are beautiful, sexy, rich, or anything else. And you certainly can't make them respond to you in the way you want them to.

Joan, a well-groomed woman in her own importing business, was desperate, after experiencing two divorces within three years to find a man who would love her. To accomplish this, she literally threw herself at every man she knew even casually. To her chagrin, not only did they not fall in love with her, but they immediately broke off the relationship they had with her.

Nothing different happened until she learned how to relax and accept the attention and love of someone else without trying to force or manipulate that person into loving her. After that, she created a healthy relationship that led to another marriage. As far as I know, she and husband number three are still very much in love with each other.

It's always amazing to me, however, how many people there are out there looking for love. Hundreds and hundreds of people attended my various relationships classes. At each one, my participants arrive in Mercedes-Benzs and in pickup trucks. I see so many different faces. Faces filled with love, hope, hunger, fear—all very moving. Underneath, they all wanted the same thing—to find the love that had been missing from their lives.

Love is Learned

I find that at any particular time we are either giving love, receiving love, or denying love.

Much of the research on love indicates that we are not born knowing how to love and be loved, we learn that. Yet, anyone who does not have enough love can learn how to create more. In addition, he or she can learn to approach love in different and changing ways.

You have many early influences that teach you about love such as your immediate family, the culture, language, movies, and advertising.

Look at how advertising influences the way you look at love. For instance, you turn on the television and you receive many love messages. "If you buy Close-Up Toothpaste, you'll get more love," is a typical message. If you look at these messages closely, you'll see that each one of them defines what makes love work and what love is suppose to be.

I find in our workshops that when you create the love you need, you can also create it the way you want it to be. One night before one of The Love of Your Life Workshops, my seven-year-old son was trying to understand what a "love workshop" was. "Is it like school?" he asked.

"Sort of."

"Does it have math in it?" he asked becoming more excited (he likes math).

"No."

"Yes it does, Mom. Love equals one hug plus two kisses. Or, love equals two hugs plus one kiss and one squeeze. It sounds like math to me!"

I had to laugh and agree because love will be what you create it to be. And as you finish this book and get to the chapter where you explore what you want in a relationship, you'll see how easy it really is.

Your Capacity for Love

On a scale from 1 to 100, what number represents your overall enjoyment of life? Think about the question for a few moments, then give your answer.

If you choose 50, then your capacity for enjoyment is 50 percent; 85 is 85 percent, and so on.

When my workshop participants do this exercise I often get all types of results. One very serious executive rated his capacity for enjoyment at about 10 percent. "All I do is work," he told me, "and I hate it."

Another rated his enjoyment of life at about 80 percent. "It's true I work all the time, too," he said, "but I love it. I get a tremendous amount of excitement from what I do." The first participant had very little capacity for love at the moment, the second had a tremendous capacity for it.

It is true that your capacity for love is equal to your capacity for enjoyment. If your capacity for enjoyment is 70 percent, then your capacity for love is 70 percent.

Your number is what your capacity is right now. Anytime you want to check your capacity for love, just repeat this exercise.

If you have a mate ask him or her what number their capacity for love is. If it is a low number at this time do not expect them to be able to give to you or receive from you more than their number indicates.

In addition to selecting a number, also notice what feelings come up when you do this exercise. Your enjoyment or love rating tells you where you stand. Your feelings help you pinpoint what is wrong. Look at the executive from my workshop again. Remember, he said, "I work all the time, I hate it." Obviously, his hate feelings were blocking his ability to enjoy and ultimately to accept love. This, he could do something about. We all have a tremendous amount of love inside us. And if we understand what the problem is, we can fix it, and increase our capacity to enjoy and to love.

Unconditional Love

The only kind of love that is truly healthy and lasting is unconditional love.

Loving unconditionally is loving someone exactly as they are without wanting or trying to change anything about them. If this sounds unattainable, it is not. Here is the key. If you create the right person for you, you won't need to change them. So many people are with the wrong partners, therefore, there will be many things they will want to change about them and they will not be able to love unconditionally.

My client Karen found herself in a relationship with a man who was quite different from herself. Karen was extremely ambitious, John wasn't. Karen was always on time, John was always an hour late for any appointment. Karen was organized, John could never find anything.

She knew this, but she decided that all she had to do to make the relationship work was to change a few of John's traits that she didn't like.

When she first mentioned these things, he said he'd try to do something about them. As she continued to nag, he became annoyed and after about the second month began to push back. Soon their arguments erupted into angry fights. John endured this turmoil for another month, then packed his bags and left.

The lesson from Karen's example is that you must either accept a person completely or reject them completely. You simply can't change anyone. When you love unconditionally, you are seeing the good, feeling the love, and focusing on what exists instead of what is missing. In addition, your ideal partner enhances the good.

With unconditional love there is a special harmony consisting of peacefulness. The peacefulness usually exists in both partners. We do not obtain that peacefulness from the relationship, we bring it with us to the relationship.

Chapter Five

Self-Love

Ultimately, love is self-approval.

—Sondra Ray

I have discovered during my years of conducting The Love of Your Life Workshops that an individual who does not know or accept who he or she is cannot love someone else. You can only love others to the degree that you can love yourself. Why? You simply cannot be there for another in ways that you cannot be there for yourself.

Let me give you an example. Julie and Don had been going together for almost a year when Don suggested they get married. They seemed to be comfortable together. Julie was a market researcher for a big firm and Don was a dentist. Julie loved Don and really wanted to make him happy, but for some reason she couldn't seem to commit. She couldn't explain why, but the prospect terrified her.

During the workshop she realized that she had a strong, unrealized need for economic self-sufficiency. She would never be satisfied, she realized, until she could stand on her own two feet. Armed with this knowledge and an old recipe of her mother's she decided to start a business selling oatmeal cookies to local restaurants.

At the end of the second month, her business was breaking even. Within a year, she had become financially independent. At this point, she realized that she could feel comfortable committing to Don. They were married the following June. While this may be an extreme case, everyone needs to know who he or she is and to be comfortable with that before they can look beyond themselves to others. As we have seen, individuals who are afraid of being who they are can never give their best selves to someone else.

It is everyone's biggest challenge to handle this problem, because many people go through an entire lifetime without knowing who they really are.

Understanding Yourself

Here are some exercises you can do to begin to know yourself better:

1. Observe yourself in new ways and from someone else's point of view. I suggest you pretend you are sitting across the room watching yourself at work, at a party, or when talking to others. Then ask yourself what kind of a person you see. Take a minute or two and make a few notes. You might say, I see a big-mouth showoff who doesn't come off as sincere. Or you might say, I see someone who is really shy and needs to let other people get closer. Whatever you find will be enlightening.

2. Pay closer attention to reality. Reality means what you really mean or are. You might say, as a worker, I didn't get a raise because the boss decided to promote his nephew . . . the reality might well be you simply aren't doing a good job. To discover this, you must ask the hard questions and be honest.

3. Achieve clarity and deeper understanding. You achieve clarity by telling the truth. Asking yourself many questions and then answering them can lead to deep-seated information. For example: What do I want to learn at this time? What is the purpose of this situation? What is another way of looking at this? Clarity and truth heals the past and helps create your future. You will only grow clearer when you tell the truth. Nothing makes you more powerful than telling the truth.

4. Answer the question, "Who am I?" into a tape recorder or in writing. Relax first, then see what comes. If you like to meditate, do that before answering. When doing this exercise, talk, or write, only about yourself. Come from your deepest self. Stay with it until you get an answer and repeat this exercise frequently.

I've given the question "Who am I?" as a homework assignment to many clients over the years. No two answers are ever the same.

Here's an example.

"I am the gentle breeze that caresses my lips on a sultry night.
I am the ray of sunshine through my window on a wintery day.
I am the shadow of hope walking beside my troubled friend.
I am love, holding the hand of the unloved.
I am a child of God."

Another said: "I am curious . . . anything will do. A spider walking across a room. Where is that spider going? What's that spider's purpose? How does that spider fit into nature? Where's that man going in such a hurry? Is he rushing home to a sick wife or child? Maybe he's rushing a report to his boss. Or maybe he's late for a date . . . I'm curious."

Even short reflections like these, if they are sincere, will help you to understand yourself.

After completing this exercise, Marie realized from the first example that she was a healer. She then began to create a whole new perspective on her life and proceeded to make some overdue changes.

Our second person, Mark, realized that he should be in a business where he could use that curiosity. As a result, he found a research job with a firm that allowed him to look into many subjects in detail.

Try this exercise with your relationship partner or with a friend: Sit facing each other. One of you begins by asking the other "Who are you?" Speak for as long as you can only talking about yourself. Then switch turns. Try to come from the deepest part of your core. See what you discover.

False Images

Another problem I see frequently is people who try to project a false image. For some reason, they think that being who they are is not good enough. It never works.

Luther D. Price said: "Be what you is, not what you ain't 'cause if you ain't what you is, you is what you ain't."

I personally feel that it's not how you love someone. It's who you are being when you love them.

Any false images of yourself that you try to project will be seen as such by anyone who *wants* to see the real you. If you put out phony images, you will not attract people who are being real.

Don't Forget Who You Are

I find that you are most powerful when you know who you are. Unfortunately, because of the pressures of modern life, it's sometimes easy to forget who we really are. As a result, we need reminders from ourself and others.

Lisa, a thirty-one-year-old advertising executive, had the reputation of being high powered and sophisticated. Her dress was always perfect and she seldom let anyone see inside her surface veneer. The truth was that Lisa grew up in the country, and really liked long walks, afternoons beside the fire, simple picnics, and romps in the yard with her golden retrievers.

Because of her projected image, however, Lisa always attracted men who were more interested in getting ahead than they were in Lisa or in simple pleasures.

After a few years of this, Lisa, decided that while she needed a professional image at work, she also needed to be herself more. During the next few months, while on a Saturday hike with a local conservation club, she met a college professor with similar interests, and soon developed a relationship that reflected the real Lisa.

Loving Yourself

Everything about you expresses how you love yourself: the way you dress, where you live, your life-style, your hair, your handshake, what you eat, who you are involved with, and all other elements of your appearance and actions.

Try this exercise. Go to a supermarket and pick out two very different types of people you see in the aisles One is well dressed, she seems to know where she is going, she treats her child with courtesy, her hair is well groomed, and she carefully selects her food. What would you say about this person?

Next pick out a negative example. You see a young woman with uncombed hair, her clothes are disheveled. She shuffles along, and keeps screaming at her child as she goes up and down the aisles. Ask yourself what kind of self-esteem and self-love does this young woman have?

What You Deserve

Other people will treat you the way you treat yourself. No one else will love you in ways that you don't love yourself.

We all know people who act like they don't deserve anything. One woman may decide she doesn't deserve a nice house; as a result, she never gets it. Or she may decide that she doesn't deserve nice clothes, a nice car, or anything else. Another woman may decide that her kids deserve material goods, but she doesn't.

To overcome this problem face your shortcomings and accept your imperfections. This allows you to overcome them and to accept and love yourself. This in turn allows you to ask for and to accept what you deserve.

The Ultimate Self-Esteem Issue

The higher you build your self-esteem, the more you will expect from a relationship. Individuals with low self-esteem are not good bets for relationship partners. I suggest that before you enter a serious relationship with anyone that you check that individual's self-esteem level. Here's how. Ask how much time that person spends in outside busy-work activities. People who stay busy with others every minute often do so to avoid spending time with themselves.

Now ask if that individual occasionally spends a whole evening by himself or herself reading or working on a project . . . or if they sometimes reserve Sunday for personal at-home projects.

Spending every waking moment with someone else or engaged in busy work often indicates low self-esteem. On the other hand, a balance of personal time and people time often indicates high self-esteem.

How Self-Esteem Affects You

The amount of self-love you can give yourself will affect everything you think, say, or do in the following ways. It affects:

- How you see the world and your place in it.
- Your ability to give and receive love.
- Your ability to grow and expand.
- How you experience happiness, joy, and personal fulfillment.
- Your health.
- Your energy level.
- Your ability to perform tasks.
- Decision-making.
- Managing your time.
- Your concentration.
- Your peace of mind.
- How productive you are.
- How creative you are.
- Your ambition.
- Your financial success.

Ways to Build Self-Esteem

Now, I would like to offer you a formula for building self-esteem that works well. Each day, review the day, acknowledge the successes you've had, and feel good about them. For instance, you might have been complimented at work, or had someone tell you how nice you look. Bask in those things for a minute.

Ken Blanchard, in *The One Minute Manager,* says that he reviews each previous day to see how he could have done things differently.

When you have high self-esteem, you will participate fully in life. Now here are some additional tips that help.

1. Acknowledge and heal the past. Let it go. Forgive yourself and others. Put it behind you and go on.

2. Keep a log of your successes. Write down each success you have. Review these successes regularly, and bask in them.

3. Talk about your successes. This helps reinforce the success in your own mind, as well as commit yourself to future success.

4. Acknowledge your personal strengths. Acknowledge that you are well organized, or that you dress well. Or that you are a problem solver. This again helps reinforce those strengths. Acknowledge the strengths of others. In the process, you will reinforce your own strengths.

5. Give to others what you want to receive for yourself. In many ways, you always get what you give. Give trust and you get trust. Be honest with another person and you tend to receive honesty.

6. Discover and support your life purpose. Some people intuitively know their life purpose, but many don't. For instance, my purpose is to help people create what they want and need in themselves and in their relationships. It is also to help individuals understand themselves and create better lives.

7. Accept yourself and others without judgment. This is almost like accepting someone without trying to change them. You must accept who you are, and who others are.

8. Treat yourself as you would someone you really loved. Think of how you treated a new relationship that you were infatuated with. You might, for instance, make sure that person has exactly what they want, go with them to do their favorite things, and go out of your way to accommodate him or her. This

is exactly how you should do it for yourself. Pamper yourself, you deserve it.

9. Ask for the support you need from others. People actually love to help. So ask for it. You'll be surprised at what happens.

10. Be truthful to yourself and others. There's nothing more painful than to have someone say he or she would love to go to an event with you, then they complain all the way through. The truth is, that person didn't want to go in the first place.

11. Take responsibility for your actions. It can be tempting to blame others for everything that goes wrong. But to build self-esteem, you must assume responsibility. For instance, if you've said you'll do something for someone and it's inconvenient, assume the responsibility and do it. Or, if you've borrowed someone's car and had an accident, it's up to you to take care of any of the problems created by your accident. Responsibility creates self-esteem.

12. Reward yourself with pleasures and gifts. Whenever you accomplish something, reward yourself. You have a report to turn in that takes extra hours. When you complete it, take yourself out to dinner as a reward for a job well done. This helps make you feel good about yourself and the job.

13. Nurture yourself each day. The best kind of nurturing is that which you do for yourself. In effect, take care of yourself.

14. Focus on the positive side. Thoughts have a tremendous influence on your self-esteem. Positive thoughts give you energy, negative thoughts pull you down.

If you find yourself thinking or saying such things as, "everything I do turns out wrong," stop right there, and change negative thoughts to positive ones.

15. Focus on your blessings and what you have, not on what you do not have.

16. Find things to be passionate about and include them in your life. Some people get passionate about baseball, others about clothes. Simply allow your natural interests to take over. This increases your enthusiasm for life.

17. Nurture within yourself the highest possible level of integrity. Integrity and self-esteem go together. Individuals who set high standards feel good about themselves. Those who don't open themselves to guilt and doubt.

18. Keep a feel-good file. Fill it with written acknowledgments and thank you cards sent to you by others. Write down compliments from others and good thoughts. Review them frequently.

19. Always honor your feelings and intuition. If you don't feel right about something, don't do it. This keeps your beliefs and actions in harmony with each other.

Here's a partner exercise to assist one another in building self-esteem:

Sit facing each other and answer the first question. Then your partner answers the same question before moving on to the next question. You can try doing this with a time limit of one, two or three minutes each or do it open-ended. Do this exercise periodically or when you feel you need some self-esteem re-enforcement.

1. Tell your partner what you like, love, and appreciate about him or her.

2. Tell your partner what his or her strengths are.

3. Tell your partner why he or she is unique.

4. Tell your partner what his or her biggest contribution to you is.

5. Tell your partner what his or her biggest contribution to your relationship is.

6. Tell your partner what his or her biggest contribution to the world is.

To help you sum up your own attitudes about self-love, answer these questions.

How would my life be different if I had higher self-esteem? How loving am I toward myself? How can I be more loving? What pain or hurt am I holding inside that is affecting my self-esteem that needs to be released? What is the most loving thing I can do for myself right now? What do I really need to make me feel happy?

Wealthy people have discovered that money does not bring happiness. Success is being happy. "The people who are truly happy are those who can successfully create and maintain relationships," says Stewart Emery, author of *Actualizations*. Those relationships will be created out of your self-acceptance first.

Silently say to yourself, "I love you."

Chapter Six

Making Choices

The strongest principle of growth lies in the human choice.

—George Eliot

At each moment you can take what you have been given or you can decide what you want. You are interested in having the love you want because you chose to read this book. You can now choose to accept or reject what comes your way.

You can see all things as problems or as opportunities, as negative or positive, as pain or pleasure.

Think of new relationships as new choices and new opportunities to learn, relearn, and to start again. Think of old relationships in this manner as well.

Over the past year, May, a personable executive secretary, has been in four different relationships. Jack, her boyfriend in the first relationship, relied on her to decide where they would go, when they would go somewhere, and with whom. This relationship allowed her to see that she needed a man who would stand on his own two feet and make his own decisions.

Her second relationship, Mick showed her that she needed someone who would respect her; the third relationship showed her that she didn't want someone who would constantly force his opinions on her; and the fourth convinced her that she could stand on her own two feet. With each relationship, May learned a lesson: she chose not to stay with that particular man as an ultimate choice and moved on. Now, May feels she has matured enough to take on a more permanent commitment. For her, her relationships have also been life-style choices.

You may think that May has a problem since she went through four relationships in just under a year. But I have discovered that there is a purpose to each relationship no matter how long it lasts, and that if you think in positive terms, you will have positive results from each new choice.

If you focus on having pleasure, your pleasure will increase. If you focus on pain your pain will increase.

Going Beyond Making Choices

You can look at your life in terms of the choices you have made or in terms of what has happened to you.

Making choices allows you to ask, "What is it that I want in a relationship?" How much do I want it? (How much responsibility am I willing to take to make it work?)

Let's say that you have met a wonderful guy who is an executive for a well-known airline. For six months you have a wonderful time. After knowing each other for three months you moved in together, bought furniture, and began decorating the house. You both paint at home in the evenings and you love to spend weekends horseback riding at a nearby ranch.

Now he drops the news that he is being transferred to Chicago and he wants you to marry him and move there. Unfortunately, you have your own wonderful job as a marketing researcher. And each day is twice as exciting as the next.

It's crunch time. Now you must ask, "What is it that I want out of this relationship? How much do I want it? Am I willing to move to make it work? Can I give up my job? Just how important is this relationship?"

There are a lot of choices to make here. And once you choose what you want and how much you want it, you must go beyond the decision making and take action.

"What do I have to do?" The actual actions taken represent your commitment to your choices. The changes you make constitute your journey.

If you decide to go to Chicago, you must actually quit your job, get married, and move. These are important choices and even more important actions. This can be the beginning of an exciting journey. And within this journey, whatever you decide, can be a lot of fun.

Increasing Your Awareness of Choices

Here's an exercise to increase your awareness of choices you can make in your life. Make a list of all things you should be doing at any one time. Most of the time, they are not going to be as exciting as your contemplated move to Chicago.

Usually, they'll be just ordinary things. Example: I should lose weight. I should weed the garden. I should repair the rip in my dress. I should call my mother, or a friend, and so forth. Take a few minutes and make this list as long as you can.

When finished, go back through your list and say each should as loud as you can. At the end of each item say, No!

This represents your choice. Remember you don't have to do anything at all . . . with each item no matter how important, you always have a choice.

Now go through your list again and change each should to I could lose weight, but I have a choice. I could weed the garden but I have a choice. I could call my mother but I have a choice. Saying "could" instead of "should" takes the pressure off and makes everything a choice. Say each one out loud, then say yes as loudly as you can. Example: I could weed the garden, but I have a choice. Yes!

After you have gone through your entire list for the third time, close your eyes and reflect on your experiences.

- What feelings came up for you? For instance, when you came to "I should lose weight" you might have experienced sadness, or guilt, or depression.
- What shoulds are running your life? I should, for instance, call my mother three or four times a week . . . I don't but I should. Shoulds often bog us down and make us feel guilty.
- What difficulties did you experience? You may find that something simple such as "I should call my mother" will make it difficult to do some of the other things you want to do, since the "should" acts as a block.
- What did you notice? You may notice that you choke or tense up. Just make a mental note of everything that happens.
- Was it easier to say could than should? When you switch to could, you'll often sigh in relief, since now instead of having a duty to perform, you have a choice.

This exercise will help create a feeling-response. Hearing no to your shoulds frees you from a duty and makes it clear you have a choice which you can change at anytime.

Now look again at the Chicago example. There are a number of possible implied shoulds here. You may think, I've been going with this person a long time, I should continue the relationship. I shouldn't be selfish and think just of myself. I shouldn't just say no.

If you try this with a partner, their role is simply to say No after each should on your list and to say Yes after each could.

Again, relationships are choices. If you have difficulty in a relationship try this exercise. Then turn the shoulds to coulds and see what happens. This will free up your thinking and allow you to make real choices about yourself, your life, and especially your relationships.

Chapter Seven

Past Relationships

*You can work at something for twenty years'
worth of valuable experience, or you can come
away with one year's experience twenty times.*
—Gwen Jackson

All of your past relationships have served your purpose and
taken you where you are right now. Up to this point, you have
needed every lesson these relationships have provided.

Think of the best relationship you have ever had. It can be
one you are in presently or one from the past. Probably this
particular relationship made you feel good and provided many
exciting times. Ask yourself: What characteristics were there
that made this relationship great?

Now, think of the worst relationship you have ever had. It
can be the one you are presently in or a relationship from the
past. This one probably provided a lot of pain. Ask yourself:
What characteristics did it have that made it terrible?

Your best and worst relationship might be the same relationship. For instance, you may have a relationship with someone
who is a lot of fun. Being with he or she is always an adventure
and the sex is fantastic. On the other hand, that person taps into
your insecurities. He or she doesn't necessarily fool around on
you, but you are always worried by the way he or she relates

to and deals with the opposite sex. Because you are insecure, it bothers you.

It is helpful to review all of your past significant relationships and to look at what did and did not work in each. This will help you affirm what you do and do not want in an ideal relationship now. Encourage your partner to look at their past significant relationships as well.

Lee, a professional model, after examining her past relationships, decided that each one had value, and that each one helped her understand what she did and did not need. One relationship convinced her that since she continually met men during her workday, she needed a partner who wasn't consistently jealous. Another showed her that she needed a partner who assumed his share of the chores. That same relationship helped her understand that she didn't want someone who expected to be entertained, but it also confirmed that she needed a partner who was considerate of her feelings.

Sometimes looking back at old relationships is a positive experience. It lets you see how far you have come. It also allows you to see what worked for you then, and why this same behavior or experience won't work now.

Often, when you are in an involved relationship, you don't clearly see what you really want. At that point, if someone flatters you, you respond. When the emotion no longer surrounds the situation, you see that person in a different light.

You can now see, for instance, that a particular individual was a great talker, had a tremendous sense of humor, and was a lot of fun. Unfortunately, he or she really didn't qualify as a possible mate since the two of you didn't communicate on the same level. You couldn't see this then, but you can now. Looking back is always a good exercise since it puts everything in perspective.

Hanging On

There often is a strong tendency to remain in a relationship that is not what you want. These relationships often bring much unhappiness and frustration. Anytime you settle for less than what you want, you lower your self-esteem.

For instance, Eileen, a long-time friend of mine, started a relationship with a man who simply wasn't right for her. Eileen wanted to attend growth events, such as seminars, lectures, and concerts. Ralph's idea of an enlightening evening was to pop open a can of beer in front of the television.

Within a short time, Eileen began to outgrow him and could hardly bear to talk to him. At that point, however, her own growth stopped.

Eileen found that she was afraid to leave. She knew it was time to make a change but she hesitated. Then, she discovered that she was pregnant. That changed everything. Now, she told herself, she had to stay. Today, Eileen hates her life, but she still lives with Ralph and has settled into a long-predictable rut.

People try to hang on to outdated and unsatisfactory relationships for many reasons, here are a few:

1. It becomes comfortable because you know each other so well. Think of it as having a pair of old shoes that were so comfortable you did not want to throw them away.

2. Looking for a new relationship seems more stressful than staying in the present one. For some people any change is upsetting.

3. You fear you will not find a new relationship. Your fears say, "Who would want you . . . you'll be alone forever." Sometimes this becomes an overriding block to ending one relationship and finding another.

4. You have an addiction to the person in the present relationship. This will be covered in greater detail later in this chapter.

5. You think that if you wait long enough, and work hard enough that the other person will change. Unfortunately, this rarely happens. And as mentioned before in this book, you should never enter a relationship with the idea that you will change someone. Accept that person's personality, or let them go completely.

6. You want to avoid the pain of breaking up and being alone. For some people, breaking up is a traumatic experience to be avoided at almost any cost since it brings out all their insecurities. For others, being alone is the worst experience they can think of. I have known individuals who panic and go all to pieces at the thought of being alone. For them, a bad relationship is preferable.

Of course, these are just a few of the excuses and reasons I have seen in my workshops. People create all kinds of excuses to not leave. Most of them are unfounded.

Personally, I believe that if you have created one relationship, you can create another one. It is often lonelier and more painful to be with the wrong person.

In addition, let me point out that someone's potential does not count. You have to go with the reality that exists in the relationship right now.

Let me show you why. After several years of building her career in a high-powered manufacturing firm, Sally found herself in a relationship where she and her partner, Jeff, fought continually.

The main problem was that while Jeff was a talented and experienced public relations professional, he couldn't seem to get along with his bosses for more than a couple of months. As a result, he continually sponged off her, something she absolutely hated.

"But," Sally rationalized, "he has tremendous potential, he just needs a little more time." After six years of putting up with this, and trying to explain her partner to her friends, she threw him out. Like many others, Sally finally discovered, that no matter how much potential a relationship has, it doesn't count if the relationship doesn't work right now.

Eventually a person leaves a relationship when he or she sees that the partner won't change, or cannot be motivated to change.

The only reason that I can see to stay in an unsatisfactory relationship would be when you are learning some valuable lessons from this relationship. For instance, you have been divorced for only a short time, and you need to learn that you have worth and value in your own right. A transitional relationship might help at this time.

This, however, works only for a limited amount of time and only if you are totally aware of the reasons for being in the relationship.

If you have had unhappy relationships in the past, I want you to do a little soul-searching. Ask yourself: Why did I stay in that relationship? Did I stay too long? Why did I finally leave? These answers should help you avoid repeating many of the mistakes in future relationships.

Patterns

A pattern in a relationship is something that an individual keeps repeating over and over again. We are always attracted to patterns in others that reinforce compulsive needs and that are most familiar to us. And we can always find someone who fits our patterns. We keep repeating our patterns until we learn the lessons they provide. Then we can move on.

Naturally, some patterns that get repeated in a relationship are positive, others are negative. Negative patterns are obstacles to love, happiness, and individual goals.

Some common repeated negative patterns are: creating a partner who is unavailable for you . . . having an alcoholic father, then marrying an alcoholic . . . always ending up abandoned . . . always choosing losers . . . dating married partners because of a fear of intimacy . . . not trusting enough . . . creating a relationship too quickly . . . having sex too soon . . . trying to change someone . . . trying to make something out of a relationship that doesn't exist.

Let me give you an example of a repeated negative pattern that ruined a life. Mark, a client of mine, always had to have a woman in his life. He had a pool cleaning business. Mark could not be alone, yet he was terrified of commitment. This meant he needed a continuing series of relationships. As a result, he would set every relationship up to fail from the very beginning. And before that relationship failed, he always had another woman ready to join him in the next one.

Mark repeated this pattern for almost forty years. He never found a committed relationship, never had a real woman friend, and never got married. In the end, he never understood what a real relationship was.

Changing Patterns

It is usually not easy to change a relationship pattern. After all, most are familiar and comfortable. To change a negative pattern you must first recognize that the pattern is destructive and then want to change it.

Most people resist changing relationship patterns to avoid discomforts, departures, and failures. But, resisting change closes doors to new people, events, things, experiences, and new arrivals into your life.

Action diminishes fear. You will grow only by taking actions to make the changes happen. You are only happy when you grow. When you are not growing, you are dying.

Some people, when they become aware that they face a problem, do something to make the needed changes. The truth is, if you want to maintain your self-love and self-esteem and obtain happiness, you must eventually do something to remedy the situation.

For other people, it takes a strong trauma such as divorce, death, or illness to initiate change. Still, others react by making negative changes or not making any change at all.

For instance, after Julie discovered she could not change her husband's messy behavior, she imitated his behavior and turned into a slob, too. They had been married for thirteen years.

Marie is an another example. One day, Marie phoned to ask about my programs. She was forty years old, alone, and sounded sad about it. I told her enthusiastically that many wonderful and interesting people attended my workshops and that they all learned a lot of new things. I added that my workshop people grew and expanded, that they had a great deal of fun, and that they formed many new friendships in the process.

For a few minutes, she did not respond. Then she replied, "I think I'll just stay home." Deep down, Marie wanted love and connection to herself and others, but was unwilling to do anything different. Unfortunately, at this stage, if you don't make changes, nothing different will ever happen.

Now, before you go any further, answer these questions: What negative patterns do you keep repeating? What are the lessons you have learned from each pattern? What do you do to change it? You will probably need to think about it before answering, but the answers to these questions can literally change your life.

If you are part of a couple these are important questions for your mate to look at as well.

Addictions

Addictions are most likely to occur when you are not clear about what you want in a relationship. Here's what happens: You meet someone, feel attracted, and begin a relationship. There is something you need that the other person becomes aware of, usually right away. You do not have to tell them what it is. It shows up on its own. Sometimes as soon as the person finds out what you need, he or she will provide it to keep you connected to them.

Rachel, a twenty-seven-year-old secretary for a law firm, met Jerome at a client party. Rachel had never been terribly popular in school, but from the very first, Jerome gave her his undivided attention. In the beginning, he called her at work, brought her flowers, ran errands for her, and gave her more attention than she had ever had. After the first month, he also started borrowing money. And by the third month, she was almost supporting him.

Rachel quickly decided this was not the relationship she wanted. In fact it was extremely destructive, but she was now hooked, she needed attention badly and he was providing it. This went on for almost a year before she finally cut him off from her income.

What you need from the other person becomes a hook to you. The hook is usually something that gives you some form of pleasure initially. Hooks are similar to drugs, that is why I call them addictions.

Even though the relationship is not what you want, you become addicted to having the hook since it meets your needs.

Some hooks can be sex, companionship, attention, security, financial support, emotional support, feeling taken care of, feeling needed, or prestige.

I know a prominent San Francisco professional who was addicted to sex. All Peter wanted out of a relationship was sex. But he would never take the time to bond or to build up trust or friendship. He would always choose women who appealed to him sexually, but who didn't have the qualities he needed in a mate. After a few months, he always moved on to someone else. As a result, to this day, he has never been able to get beyond his sexual addiction to create a long-term relationship.

I have also had men clients in my workshop whose egos caused them to be addicted to beauty. They always seem to have a string of beautiful women around them, but never a committed or deep relationship.

Champagne

Just okay relationships are like drinking a glass of wine. The wine is just okay. Then if champagne comes along your glass is already full and there is not any place to put the champagne. In your heart you want champagne because champagne is the best.

Your glass needs to be empty to be available for the champagne. In other words, if you want to create an ideal relationship, you must be willing to keep your glass empty for it.

With each relationship your energy changes. If you are in a great relationship, your energy is positive and high. If you are in the wrong relationship, your energy goes down and is negative.

Remember, positive energy is what attracts people, negative energy repels. I believe that it is better to keep a glass empty than half full. Which simply means that you must always be emotionally available to have the relationship you really want.

Sandy, an attractive high school teacher and a client of mine, spent almost three years in a relationship that was what she called satisfactory, but not exciting. She enjoyed going places with her partner, but she couldn't really talk to him, or get into the deep issues that interested her. While nothing happened to provoke her, she came home one weekend and told her partner it was over.

From that very moment on she began to feel better about herself, and develop new enthusiasm for life. Two weeks later, she met Tom, another teacher at a friend's party. That first night they sat in the friend's living room, laughing and talking about their ideas until four o'clock in the morning. Each topic one of them brought up seemed to stimulate the other. Within a few weeks the whole tone of Sandy's life changed. Now it was exciting and vibrant. Sandy realized that she had found this relationship quite by accident. Yet, if she hadn't cut off her other relationship, she wouldn't have been available for the party. Nor would she have been able to tap the excitement she now felt.

The moral of this chapter is: You become what you surround yourself with. Around wine, you will be wine. Around champagne, you will be champagne.

Chapter Eight

Parents

What God is to the world, parents are to their children.

—Philo

Your mother and father are your most important relationship role models although the message is always different for each individual. Parents influence our thoughts, attitudes, conditioning, judgments, and initial patterns. Through them we learn some of our most significant lessons.

One individual, for instance, may have grown up in a loving home where his or her mother or father respected each other, and where the atmosphere was always supportive. Another may come from an alcoholic home where the father staggered in night after night and fought with the mother. Still, another man or woman grew up in a home where the mother found fault with the father, and the father stayed away as much as possible.

Other early authority figures such as aunts and uncles, older siblings and cousins, grandparents, schoolteachers, and neighbors have also been relationship role models.

Let's do a little exercise. List five things that you do within your present or most recent relationship. For instance, you may insist that your partner help with the housework . . . treat you with respect . . . let you know when he or she intends to be late . . . take time out whenever you have an argument . . . and use good manners in the house.

Or you may scream at your partner . . . stop talking when you get mad . . . slam the door and walk out of the room . . . stay away from home some nights . . . and talk to your mate politely only when it is to your advantage.

Look to see which of these activities may have been modeled initially by your mother or father.

When Parents Offer Unconditional Love

My mother mastered unconditional love and taught me about it my whole life. Although she had a tough time in childbirth, I have been told that when I was born, my mother laid me across her belly and whispered to me, "I will never let you down." Since that time, she has been my best friend. Mother always looked for the positive and the good stuff, and I never heard her say anything bad about anybody. And although she was crippled for years with arthritis, I never heard her complain.

As a result of my mother's example, I believe it is no accident that I became a "love counselor!"

What your parents thought of you affects how you love yourself. All through my childhood my mother always told me I was wonderful and that I could do anything I set my mind to. As a result, I have self-worth and easily take on new challenges.

Just as your parents taught you how to be in the world, you will teach your children. They will copy much of what you do. When my son was seven years old, we went into a 7–11 Store. He bought two pieces of bubble gum and asked the clerk for a receipt. He had seen me ask for many receipts for my various purchases. How my son sees me in my romantic relationships to others will reflect on his future love partners.

Thelma and Sam

Thelma and Sam, my parents and role models, met at a party. It was love at first sight. Sam drove Thelma home. While driving across the George Washington Bridge, he said with passion, "Thelma, if you don't say you will marry me, I will drive right off this bridge!"

According to my mother, since she had no choice, she said, "YES!"

A month later, they eloped to Atlantic City and brought Thelma's mother with them. Trying to dissuade Sam from marrying so hastily, his family got him fired from his job. The point did not sink in and nothing could stop the couple.

I have never seen two happier people in my life. I learned a lot from them.

Growing up in a loving, warm, and affectionate atmosphere taught me what was possible in relationships. As a result, my standards have been high.

Some lessons my parents taught me were:

- The importance of assessing situations rather than being too impulsive.
- Spontaneity can bring excitement to relationships.
- Risk-taking pays off.
- Commitment to what you believe in boasts personal power.
- The equality of power between men and women is not automatic.
- Family support and bonding has strong impact on future achievements.
- Stubborness is a form of control.
- The heart can be stronger than the mind.

- Intuition is to always be listened to.
- Inner strength can require much work.
- Insecurities prevent self-confidence.
- A sense of humor goes a long way.

Some of those parental lessons have been easy and some pretty tough. Many people have had very painful experiences with their parents and/or they have unfinished business with them. I'm so thankful to Thelma and Sam for their shortcomings and their love.

Here are a few positive lessons some of my clients have learned from their parents:

- Doing a lot of things together helps bring solidity to a marriage.
- Being devoted means being affectionate.
- Doing a lot of little things for each other reinforces love.
- Compromising is necessary.
- Doing your best is an expression of your feelings.
- Being honest brings positive rewards.
- Being present for your children reinforces love and caring.

Your Lessons

Think back to your own mother and father. What positive principles did you learn from them that you now use in your own relationships? I suggest you identify both the positive and negative patterns as you make your list. If you have a mate, ask what lessons were learned from his or her parents.

As you work with your present relationships, the trick is to retain the positive lessons learned from your parents and eliminate the negative ones. While this takes work, it's easier than creating entirely new patterns since those learned from your parents are already deeply ingrained in your psyche.

Unresolved Parental Issues

Most adults know that they have a number of issues they have never completely resolved with their parents. Here are some of the unresolved parental issues I hear mentioned about in my workshops: My parents didn't say I love you enough . . . my parents didn't give me enough freedom . . . they were too strict . . . they still don't treat me like an adult . . . they won't let me do anything for myself . . . we still can't talk to each other . . . and many more.

What I find is that most unresolved issues that you have with your parents will turn up over and over again in your present relationships.

Let's say that you feel your parents never treated you fairly and wouldn't listen to your side of arguments. You certainly don't look for a mate who will treat you like this, but if it happens, you will react with supersensitivity toward it. That is, you will probably overreact.

Or, say your mother constantly yelled at you, and you resented it, but you could never come to terms with her. Again, you certainly won't look for a mate who does this, but you will overreact if this comes up. The same will be true of any other unresolved problems left over from your parents.

If you like, you can now use your present relationships to resolve these issues intentionally rather than waiting to be pushed up against them when they show up.

How? Look at the relationship you have or have had with each of your parents. What unresolved issues do you now have with your mother? What unresolved issues do you have with your father? Make a list for each.

Examples of Unresolved Mother Issues:
She always favors my sister over me.

She does not give me any physical affection.
She does not trust me.
She abandoned me when I was young.
She is disrespectful of me.
She is always too busy for me.

Examples of Unresolved Father Issues:
He does not see me for who I really am.
He is jealous of my boyfriends.
He tries to control me.
He wants me to be just like him.
He expects too much of me.
He does nothing to encourage me to succeed.

Now, which of these issues do you see in your present relationships?

When you identify them, begin to view them as lessons for your present relationships, just as you have with the other lessons presented in this book. You will discover that there is a close tie between the issues you are working on today, and your unresolved parental issues . . . all of them are waiting to be resolved as you learn today's lessons and create your ideal relationship.

Chapter Nine

Fear

Nothing in life is to be feared. It is only to be understood.

—Marie Curie

We experience many different emotions such as sadness, anger, guilt, anxiety, hopefulness, hurt, satisfaction, depression, confusion, and many others. But the two basic ones are love and fear. They are the most powerful feelings we all have.

People have killed for love, traveled around the world for love, and are motivated by love on the very deepest level of their souls. People have died out of fear, and hidden their whole lives from fear-filled neurosis. Other themes everyone experiences in some form are birth and death, success and failure, joy and sorrow. But love and fear are the dominating themes of our lives and part of all the other themes as well.

Your biggest desire is to have a good relationship with another person, to have love. Unfortunately, often your biggest fears also revolve around relationships. While you want love more than anything, you can fear it more than anything.

For instance, think of the last time you met someone you really liked. You were extremely excited. At the same time you said to yourself, "Maybe that person won't like me." Now you have created "love" and "fear" at the same time.

The truth is you can experience both love and fear simultaneously. The stronger emotion will take over the weaker one. For many people, love wins out, but for others their fears override everything else, almost at once.

I used to write a column that drew many responses. I want to share three with you.

The first one from Marian said, "I love the man I'm going with, but I become terrified when I consider spending a lifetime with him. Sometimes these two emotions become so strong, I want to run away and hide."

Another from Keith said, "I've been going with my girlfriend for two years now, and she's pressuring me to get married. While I love her I seem to find every excuse in the world to put her off. To tell the truth I'm afraid if I tell her no, she'll leave, and if I say yes, I'll leave. Believe me, it isn't funny."

Finally, Nancy wrote to say, "I have too many present commitments and responsibilities. What can I do about lack of time for a relationship?" This letter is also a manifestation of fear, since being busy is a way of avoiding relationships.

If you find yourself with both strong attractions and strong fears at the start of a new relationship it's time to look within yourself. Ask, Why do I want this relationship? Mentally click off the reasons. I want someone to spend time with. A relationship makes me feel good. I need someone to talk to and so forth. Now start focusing on each of these reasons. Hopefully, they will soon begin to override the fears.

To see if you want to move toward or away from someone, notice if your feelings for the person arise from love or fear. You can usually tell. As a woman, for instance, you may enjoy talking to that new man and like the way he pays attention to you. But you don't like the fact that he continually looks at the other women in the room, or that he leaves you alone for long periods of time.

Try to put a label on each of these feelings. Which ones are love and which are fear? Love indicates you are going toward the person, fear indicates backing away. You will, of course, react differently with every person you meet, unless your pattern involves love addiction or fear of intimacy.

The desire to love or to enjoy another person is strong, but there is usually some degree of fear about it. In addition, not only do you have these two feelings within yourself, so does the other person.

What Are Fears?

Fears are only your thoughts, usually based on illusion. They are not real because thoughts exist only in your mind. Sometimes, however, your present fears are based on what actually happened in the past. If your last three relationships have turned sour, you will probably fear the next one will also. If you have a track record of new acquaintances not calling you back, you will probably fear the next one won't either. Fortunately, about 90 percent of what we worry about never happens.

We also often project fears to others, as issues we are working on at the time. For instance, you are trying to teach yourself to trust people. During that time one of your fears will be trust.

Finally, you will often create what you fear will happen. Being afraid of rejection will create rejection. Being afraid you will lose creates losing.

Valerie, a vivacious and beautiful 26-year-old medical student, had a terrible fear of going out with Mr. Right one time and then never seeing that person again. "Every time I heard the words, 'I'll call you,' " she said, "I panicked and assumed that I'd never hear from that person again. And you know what? I usually didn't."

This went on until Valerie finally convinced herself that somehow she was telegraphing her fears to her dates, and literally scaring them off ahead of time. After turning her fears around, life returned to normal.

Fear Visualization

Fears are really a form of visualization. Used in positive ways, visualization can be extremely useful. Used in negative ways it can be a self-fulfilling prophecy.

Many athletes use mental visualizations of themselves winning before a competition. In one experiment, two groups of basketball players were asked to shoot foul shots for twenty minutes before a contest. The first group was told to sit on the bench and see themselves shooting baskets (visualization). The second group was told to practice for 20 minutes. In the actual contest, those who practiced visualization made more shots than those who practiced shooting baskets.

I have also seen this occur many times in my own workshops. I frequently hold different contests in my many classes. Surprisingly, most of the winners know they are going to win long before we finish the contest. "I knew I'd win before we started," one told me. "I saw it in my mind."

What you must do in real life is to visualize the positive and to avoid visualizing fears into reality.

What Are You Afraid Of?

There are many different fears in relationships. The two biggest ones are "you are going to lose the relationship" and "you are going to lose your personal space." Fear of being separated is fear of losing the relationship. If you try to hold on, you feel powerless. Other fears include fear of intimacy, fear of rejection, fear of being abandoned, fear that you are not good enough, fear that the other person will see the real you, and more.

Fear of losing your personal space is fear of losing your personal freedom. Another thing to remember is that all fears are fear of loss. If you look at the fears I have listed above you will see that every one of them is about loss, fear of rejection, fear of being abandoned, and so forth.

While I believe that all fears are fear of loss, some other basic reasons why people experience the most common fears are:

- Being hurt.
- Fear of the unknown.
- Not taking enough risks.
- Lack of self-esteem.
- Lack of self-confidence.
- Lack of people in their life who provide love, nourishment, and support.
- Lack of experience.
- Negative attitudes.
- Misconceptions about success.
- The necessity to learn the lessons connected to the fear.
- Lack of success-oriented role models.
- Not trusting that the Universe provides for their highest good.
- Past mistakes that were made.
- Not feeling free to express themselves freely.
- Loss of control.
- An unbalanced life.
- Low energy.

If you really do want a relationship but your fears are stopping you, find out what you might be afraid of losing if you had a relationship. Instead of losing things in your life, with an appropriate partner all the wonderful things would be enhanced. Are you losing more by not having it? Fears provide us with tremendous opportunities to open ourselves up in ways we need to provide more satisfaction and healing in relationships.

Now, I want to ask you to make a list of all your fears about relationships. Next to each fear, write down what you will lose.

Example: I fear he/she will try to change me.
I will lose my individuality.

I fear I'll become bored.
I will lose time.

I fear I will be lonely.
I will lose companionship.

I fear the other person will yell at me.
I will lose my courage.

I fear my partner will expect me to do all the work.
I will lose my inner peace and become angry instead.

I fear I won't find someone new if this marriage ends.
I will lose my confidence.

I fear I am not good enough for the other person.
I will lose self-esteem.

I fear he/she will control me.
I will lose my self-identity.

I fear he/she will cheat on me.
I will lose trust.

Take some time for this one, search your soul and list all your possible fears. Bringing them out in the open often makes you see if they are unfounded. Do this exercise alone first and then with your partner or with a friend. The things that you fear you will lose are the areas that you will need to provide for yourself.

To further check out your balance of fears in relationships, ask yourself: How much of my feelings are based on need and how much are based on wanting to extend love? This helps balance the two. What is the payoff for having it be this way?

Overcoming Fears

There are two ways of living life. You can let your fears stop you from having what you want or you can ignore these fears and advance anyway. When you let fears interfere, you block your own personal growth. But when you act in a positive manner, you open up to more love for yourself and from others.

Each time you move beyond a fear, your capacity for loving increases. Now look at what this means. Each time you overcome fear, you grow. This means that, in reality, you can welcome fears, not avoid them because each one represents an opportunity you can take advantage of. Overcoming each new fear brings the opportunity of more love. Only love can unblock fear and only fear can block love.

You must confront your fears to move steadily forward. As you move toward your fears, they become smaller and as you move away from them they become bigger.

To overcome fears, get them out in the open as soon as possible. That is, identify them, communicate them to yourself and others . . . then let go. If you have a toothache and fear going to the dentist, you will overcome this experience only by going through the experience.

Fears are really friends you can use as important lessons in your quest to create the relationship or relationships that you really want. Learn this, and fear will no longer be your enemy.

Chapter Ten

Communication

Once a human being has arrived on this earth, communication is the largest single factor determining what happens to him in this world.
—Virginia Satir

Everyone of us wants to hear the words "I love you." In fact, some people will do and say almost anything to get someone else to say these words to them.

Sometimes a man or woman will say "I love you," to another person just to hear the words said back.

While everyone understands the general meaning of the words, each person who uses them may mean something different. For instance, "I love you" can mean: "I want somebody to escort me to the company dinner" . . . "I am sexually attracted to you but confused" . . . "I'm really lonely and you're paying attention to me" . . . "Your mind turns me on" . . . "You fill a need for me," and much more.

In addition, you might ask yourself does this mean "I love you" at this moment? Forever? or When?

Since "I Love You" means something different to each person, it must be made clearer through communication.

For instance, Nancy, a high school principal, fell in love with Bob at first sight. He was, he told her, an out-of-work advertising executive who had a number of terrific job offers and would be back to work shortly.

Two weeks later, Bob told her he loved her. A few days after that he borrowed two thousand dollars to help him find a job. During the next six weeks Nancy gave him another three thousand dollars. He professed his love but came to see her less and less. One night, Bob called to say he wouldn't be there that evening because he had set up a last-minute interview. Suspicious, Nancy drove to his house and found him with another woman.... The last thing she heard as she went down the stairs was, "I love you."

Because someone says, "I love you," does not mean that they do. Their actions toward you actually explains what they mean. Words are cheap!

The Importance of Communication

Eighty-five percent of your success depends on your ability to get along with others. I believe that whenever any disagreement occurs between two people, you can always trace the root cause to poor communication. You make changes, solve problems, and turn fears around through communicating with someone else.

In going through her checkbook, my client Donna discovered that her husband Ralph had written a check for one thousand dollars, but he hadn't said a word about it. She didn't mention it, but from then on she paid special attention to everything he did.

Whenever she went to his office she noticed he and his secretary whispered together and kept glancing at her. She kept quiet, but when she discovered a check made out to his secretary, that was it. Donna packed her clothes and got ready to move out. If he wanted the secretary instead of Donna, well, Ralph could have her.

At this point Ralph came through the front door with a package that turned out to be a diamond bracelet he had been planning to give her for their anniversary. Since he spent much of each week out of town, he had asked his secretary to handle the details. The check was the remainder Ralph owed on the bracelet.

It was all a terrible mistake that could easily have been avoided with a little communication.

Communication will often make the difference between success or failure in your relationships. Growing, expanding, loving, and nurturing are connected to your communication process. As you express your needs and feelings, your energy becomes freed up and you will be more productive, intuitive, and creative.

Ask for What You Want

The best way to get what you want is to ask for it. Listen to what your partner wants. That is also how you get your needs met. If your mate does not act the way you need them to, then you must tell them.

Gloria enjoyed musicals, but put off asking her new boyfriend George to take her because she was afraid he might not enjoy them. In their conversations she discovered he was a bluegrass fan. She offered to go with him to a bluegrass concert, then asked if he would go with her to a series of musicals. The answer was yes, the result of listening and asking.

Think about all the things you want, but are afraid to ask for. How much do you want them? Unfortunately, if you want something badly within a relationship that you are not asking for, stress begins to build and fester between you and your partner.

Start now and list those things that you feel you need in your relationship. If you have not communicated these needs to your partner, do so. Some will be taken care of almost immediately, others must be worked out between you and your partner over a period of time.

Relationship Honesty

It is extremely important for both men and women to be completely open and honest about the type of relationship each wants. Some individuals are looking for a marriage, some a live-in relationship, others a committed partnership or a limited friendship. Sometimes couples need to explore and clarify how their partnership is presently meeting their needs, look at what is missing or learn how to strengthen, support, and preserve what they have together.

If your goal is to have a monogamous marriage and your new friend has just been divorced and wants to date a variety of people, it is unlikely that the relationship will work in the long run. In addition, if you find that your overall relationship goals are different from that of your potential partner, and you continue anyway, you are setting yourself up for failure.

Let me share an example with you. Harry and Flo, both clients of mine, started dating each other as a healing relationship, after they both lost long-term significant relationships. Three months later, the healing was complete and it was time to reevaluate their relationship. They were both hesitant to bring up the subject because they were each afraid that the other wanted more from them than they wanted to give.

Each thought if they brought it up, they would lose what they had. But Flo finally got up the courage to tell Harry that she felt it was much too early to make a real commitment. He gave a big sigh of relief and told her that is exactly how he felt but was afraid to tell her. After that, both relaxed and began to enjoy the relationship they had at the moment. This particular relationship ended with the two partners breaking up a year later. But both agreed it helped them grow tremendously. Other partners in my classes, however, have gone through relationships like this and ended up married within a year or two.

Of course, even if you are being wonderfully honest about what you want, the other person may not know what he wants at this time. By bringing the subject up, he may begin to examine his own feelings.

If he is not as clear about it as you, it is possible that relationships are not as important to him as they are to you. Find this out.

Another pitfall is that some people lie about what they want. They may be telling you what they think you want to hear or they could be deceiving themselves.

In either case, watch what their "actions" are. Watch to see how much time and energy they spend on you. Their actions are far more meaningful than words.

One other word of warning, do not ever wait for someone else's goal to change. If their mind is made up, it doesn't matter how wonderful, beautiful or handsome, sexy, or rich you are. You could wait for many years and finally wind up frustrated. You have to look at what-is now, and forget about future potential. Future doesn't matter in terms of people's relationship goals. It's what's happening right now.

Being honest in all areas, however, makes it so much easier to connect with the right person from the beginning.

Despite the problems we've discussed about honest communication, connecting with new people and reconnecting with our longer-standing partners is a wonderful adventure and challenge. It keeps us feeling alive and growing, offers a way to put excitement and adventure in our lives, and most important, it gives us a chance to meet and be with those people with whom we can "create the relationship" we really want.

Assumptions

Has anyone ever expected you to be able to read their mind? When someone expects this and you cannot, he or she may become angry. "I thought you would know that!"

When people meet you for the first time they may make assumptions about you just on your appearance. They decide immediately that you are a happy person, a sad one, or someone who is unfriendly. That may not be the case at all. For instance, if they assume you are unfriendly, you could simply be tired, and, for the moment, are a little standoffish.

Husbands and wives often have this "implied-communication" problem. For instance, your mate comes home every night and plops in front of the television until bedtime. What you want is a little conversation. But you are never going to get it unless you ask. The other person can't read your mind. Yet a lot of couples have broken up because of just such a scenario.

In another case, Fred began to assume that his wife of three years, Nora, would know, without being told, what he needed. As long as his wants weren't too great, she accommodated him. But one afternoon he stalked through the front door and demanded to know where his suitcase was.

"What suitcase?" his wife asked.

"What suitcase?" he screamed. "Half an hour ago my boss told me I had two hours to catch a plane to Europe. If you loved me you would have known and had my suitcase ready."

Furious, she stalked out of the house leaving him to pack his own suitcase. When he returned from the trip she had completely cleared out. They are back together again . . . but the suitcase is still a very sore point.

Do not assume anyone knows or understands anything that

you did not say or did not communicate to them. Now, let me give you one more example.

While I was out of town, my friend Lance painted my office. He slept there overnight and gave my phone number to someone he had an appointment with. He missed this appointment, and two days later, the person he stood up called and left him a twenty-minute screaming message on my answering machine.

I returned and got Lance's message. Whoever left it assumed that this was Lance's office and that he would be there to receive the message. Instead, I became the victim of an assumption.

Communication Connection Map

Every issue in relationship is connected to you and to each other. All the connecting lines in Figure 1 represents the communication link that connects you to your learning, growing, and changing each of those issues.

Look at the Communication Connection Map. You will see that the issues that come up in a relationship include trust, risking, commitment, fears, self-esteem, and more represented in the circles. I want to impress upon you here that the only way to change any of these issues within the relationship is to communicate with your partner about them.

Suppose one of the issues you seem to have a problem with is **risk.** You are in a relationship that you want to keep, but you don't **love** the other person and you **feel** you need to be honest about that. Unfortunately, when you do, you risk losing him or her. Or the other person might become angry.

Again, no change or growth can occur until you communicate. The connecting lines between these issues and between you represents the communication that needs to take place once you are ready for something different to occur. There are some guidelines here, however. Be sincere, honest, have empathy for the other person, and come from a loving place. You might say,

COMMUNICATION CONNECTION MAP

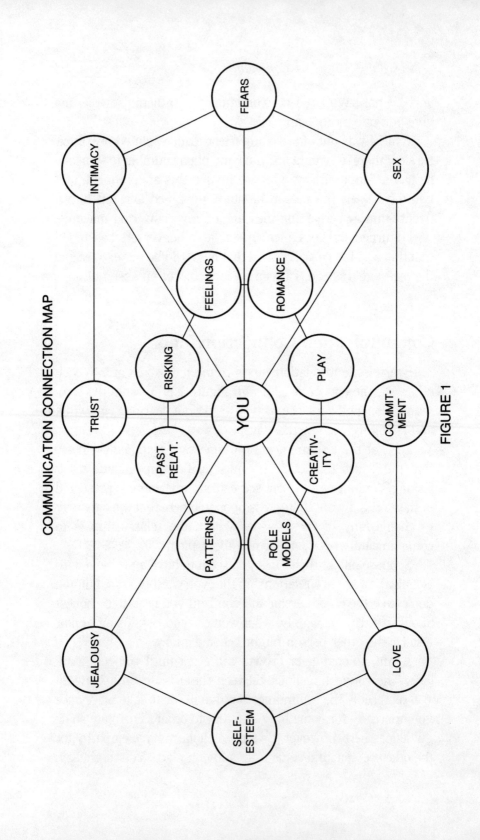

FIGURE 1

"You're a wonderful person. You are kind and considerate and I really appreciate that. I'm flattered that you love me, but I don't feel the same thing. However, I love our relationship, and I would like to keep it as it is." You can say something like this, or whatever you really mean.

Look at the chart again, decide which issues need changing, then resolve to start working on them by communicating your needs about each to your partner. Remember the lines between the issues are the reminders to communicate to make the necessary changes.

When you begin to work on issues, you will discover many are interconnected. If you feel **jealous** when your partner spends time with a **past relationship** you begin to stop **trusting,** you **fear** there is someone else in your partner's life and your **self-esteem** is affected, resulting in a lack of **intimacy,** breaking the **commitment.** Don't try to work on them all at once. Pick one issue at a time and work on that. When you are satisfied, move to the next.

How You Communicate

The words that you use are important but your inner purpose always speaks louder than words . . . because no communication is effective unless it comes from the heart.

When you communicate from your head, you must integrate it with your heart to completely connect with others. You can do this by staying in touch with your feelings and by allowing them to come out.

Conversely, you always need to listen to what someone is saying beyond their words. By keeping an open heart you will tune in to another person's mood, feelings, and attitude. Of course it's not always that easy. I once saw a young man and young woman shopping in an exclusive women's shop. Apparently, he had promised to buy her a present. She looked at a sweater she obviously considered perfect. But it was more than their budget allowed.

After that you could see in her eyes that nothing she looked at matched up. Fortunately, her young man could see it, too. After a short time, they started to leave without buying the sweater she wanted. But before they got out the door he sent her ahead, while he went back. A few minutes later, I saw him pay for the sweater. Her body language and her inner-emotional communication told him how much she wanted that first sweater . . . and he had responded. While this is an example of a material need . . . we also communicate deep feelings about love, hate, and more . . . all on the same inner level.

"Man cannot live by words alone, despite the fact that sometimes he has to eat them," Adlai Stevenson once remarked.

Communication Process Exercise

In this section, I want to give you an exercise you can try with your partner. In practice I have found it makes a real difference. You will need to set aside a regular time each week for yourself and your partner.

Each partner should prepare ahead and make three lists.

List Number One: Write down all the things that you appreciate about your partner. They must all be something that is positive and that works for you in the relationship.

> *Example:*   John is trying hard to communicate clearly.
> John is usually on time.
> John is very affectionate.
> John is considerate.

List Number Two: Write down all the things that you fear about your relationship. These are things that might be holding you back from having a closer connection.

Example: I fear that you are attracted to Lisa.
I fear that I will have to travel for my job so much that we will not have enough time together.
I fear that I am not romantic enough.

List Number Three: Write down all the miscellaneous things you would like to discuss with your partner. These could be all types of ideas and thoughts about almost anything.

Example: I decided to go to a new dentist.
What plans do you have for Thanksgiving?
Jean gave me a terrific new recipe for chicken and I would like to try it out on you. Is Thursday evening okay?

When you meet, one of you reads your list number one. When finished, the other person also reads his or her list number one. Next, one of you reads list number two. Leave time in between for discussion and resolution. Repeat the procedure as with list number one. Do the same for list number three.

This weekly meeting helps both of you communicate problems, elicits feedback, turns fears around, and gives you a chance to discuss additional items with each other.

If you find anything that is difficult to talk about during the week, discuss these in your weekly meetings. Within a short time I find that these meetings help create a better atmosphere between the partners, closer connections, and deeper bonding.

Closer Connections

To achieve closer connections, you must also be willing to share your deepest and innermost feelings. Not only does sharing bring you closer, it opens you up to your feelings in new ways.

I sometimes get concerned in counseling when I find couples

whose communications about feelings stay on a surface level. That is a sure sign they are not sharing deeply enough by taking enough risks, or by dealing with fears, disappointments, and negatives. The more honestly you can open up to someone the more satisfying the relationship will be. When you are afraid of loss, you tend to withhold your communication and that is exactly when the relationship needs strengthening.

Sally and Bill met at one of my workshops and quickly became close to each other. They spent every waking moment together for the next two months. The next time I saw Sally, however, she looked pale and drained.

"I haven't told Bill yet about my daughter Myrna and I'm terrified," she told me. "I know he'll leave me once he discovers I have a child . . . he has often told me he likes being spontaneous, and heavens knows it's hard to be spontaneous when you are tied down."

"You should have let him know the first night," I advised her. "Do it now, even if you lose him."

Two weeks later I ran into Sally again. She was smiling from ear to ear. "I told him," she said, "and he was delighted. I don't know what I was thinking of. I went through all that fear and frustration for nothing."

That's one type of problem that occurs because of not communicating deeper inner problems. Here's another. A couple I counseled, Beth, a technical writer and Charlie, a self-employed contractor, initially seemed like they didn't have a problem in the world. The first thing I asked them to do was to write down all the problems they were working on, and the questions they had. Beth told me, "we don't have any problems."

When they came to my office and started talking I discovered there were lots of issues between them. The most serious was that he had a three-year-old son from a previous relationship. The mother wanted him to stay out of the child's life.

The problems simply hadn't come out before with Beth and Charlie because neither one of them wanted to rock the boat.

A few days later Beth called me to say they were breaking up and she was flying back to Chicago, her hometown. What hadn't been talked about proved too much for them. If you don't get things out on the table in the beginning, so much resentment builds up over a period of time that it often destroys the relationship.

My suggestion to everyone is that you spend fifteen to thirty minutes every day communicating your feelings with your partner. It must be a two-way sharing. Ask the other person how they are feeling and what they need from you. Give each other feedback and make sure you understand each other.

Human contact is an exquisite opportunity as well as a challenge. It can be as much fun and self-expressive as you want it to be. For instance, you might start by running through a list of your feelings. Happy, sad, depressed, elated, and so forth and let the other person respond. If you would like to feel differently, what do you need to make the changes happen? The point is to share and to clear your mind, so get started in any way that works, and see where it goes.

Communication Checklist

Here are a series of questions I use to determine how well two people are communicating in a relationship. Simply run through the questions and write out the answers on a separate sheet of paper.

- How openly do you express your love verbally? Physically? Through actions?
- How often do you check with your partner about his or her feelings?
- How do you respond when he or she is distressed?
- What needs haven't you expressed? What feelings have you not shared?

- Are your communications clear to your partner?
- Do you make sure you understand what your partner has told you before you reply?
- Do you ask questions to clear up misunderstandings?
- Do you use too many words to get your meaning across? Too few words?
- Do you listen with your full attention or are you busy thinking of your response?
- Can you allow your partner to finish or do you repeatedly interrupt?
- What frustrates you when you communicate?
- How do you feel about your communication?
- What bothers you about your partner's communication?
- What stops your communication?
- What is the most difficult for you to ask for? What do you do when it comes up? What can you do differently?
- What keeps you from asking for what you need?
- Do you want to be right or do you want to be in a relationship?

To evaluate these questions, decide whether each answer is positive or negative. Then set aside negative issues to work on.

As an example, let's take the question: What frustrates you when you communicate? Your answer: "I'm frustrated because I can't figure out what I am angry about when I have an argument or discussion with my partner. I never know what I really mean until later on. That way I don't really get to say what I need to say. It is driving me wild."

Now that you've identified this, go back and work on it with your partner. Reopen the communication to complete what you didn't say the first time. You can do this in person, by writing that person a letter, or by telephone.

Again, don't try to correct all the negatives at once, but identify them, work on one thing at a time until you are satisfied, then go on to the next.

Chapter Eleven

Risking

*The fishermen know that the sea is dangerous
and the storm terrible, but they have never found
these dangers sufficient reason for remaining
ashore.*

—Vincent van Gogh

To keep your relationship alive, growing, and improving you
must take risks. Relationships that run into trouble can often be
saved if one or both partners are willing to risk. For instance,
let's say both of you are afraid of commitment. However, one
partner wants a committed relationship more than the other. As
a result, you've been fighting about this for weeks. Of course the
riskiest thing you can do is to throw caution to the winds, forget
the fears, and get married. Risky? Yes, but sometimes bold and
risking moves are really the only thing that makes sense.

Without taking risks, your relationships stand still, become
inactive, and possibly boring. When you always know what will
happen, you will soon begin to take the people you are close to
for granted. This eliminates the spontaneity and often ends up
killing the relationship.

Taking risks can mean many things: Taking a chance on
someone you just met . . . sharing negative feelings . . . letting
yourself go in front of other people . . . taking a trip to another
city on the spur of the moment . . . asking for a raise . . . quitting
your job . . . starting a business . . . moving from one city to

another . . . buying a car you can't afford . . . revealing your past to your partner . . . and more. We usually think of risks as doing something we have not done before because the results are uncertain.

If being a little offbeat, or letting yourself be wild and crazy are a part of your personality, then those parts need to come out sometimes. Suppressing any part of your self-expression will close down a part of you and in the end can inhibit or destroy your relationships. Relationships have to remain open in order for them to move forward.

For instance, most of the time twenty-eight-year-old Bob was rather subdued and businesslike. At the office, he kept to himself and did his job efficiently. At a party or in a group of people, however, he became an extrovert. He introduced himself to everyone in the room and engaged anyone who wanted to talk in conversation. Shellie, his fiancée, hated it. On every occasion she insisted he become more laid back. After a while, Bob gave up and withdrew into himself.

The problem was that Shellie was not open in the beginning of the relationship about how she expected Bob to behave. She was afraid to risk his reactions to her stiff demands.

When Bob risked by being himself, the life of the party, Shellie wanted to control him and his actions. Shellie was actually afraid to take these risks herself. As a result, he broke off the engagement and disappeared from Shellie's life. Taking risks is being who you are and it is only by being who you are that you can have a healthy and productive relationship. People who risk get closer to their relationship goals whether they win or lose.

In general, the more risks you take that are compatible with your personality, the better off the relationship will be.

Fear of Taking Risks

The reason most of us do not take risks is that we want security and we fear taking risks will destroy that. The most common fears are:

• Fear of loss—you could lose the relationship, your self-respect, control of your partner or the situation, and control of your emotions.
• Fear of rejection—you need to be accepted by having the love and approval of another.
• Fear of the unknown—there is always an element of fear in doing anything you haven't done before.
• Fear of revealing yourself—the fear is that the other person will reject you or that you are not good enough.
• Fear of pain and hurt—everyone fears pain, usually unnecessarily.
• Fear of change—this is a tremendous fear for some people. I have known individuals who literally panic at the thought of change and remain immobilized until the need for it has passed.

"While we all fear that we'll be hurt if we care, it's better to take a chance on love, than to wish, when we've lost the chance, that we had." Unknown

Fear of Rejection

When we fear rejection, we generally develop a number of negative feelings. Actually, rejection can be a blessing. When someone rejects you, that means you do not belong with them anyway. Think about this for a minute. When someone rejects you, they are rejecting a part of your personality. The only way you can continue that relationship is to change. There is nothing wrong with making changes, but that is your decision alone, not someone else's.

Think of rejection as an opportunity. Why? Because when you are rejected by someone who doesn't want you, you are then freed up to be with someone who does.

Let me give you an example that shows this clearly. Helen was a pleasant woman who had the habit of bursting into song whenever something happened that delighted her. This habit embarrassed Leon, her boyfriend of a year, because he never knew when she might start singing. He warned her about it several times, then blew up when she started singing in the middle of a company gathering. "I've had it," he told her, "we're finished." And on that, he stalked away leaving her in the middle of a staring crowd.

She stood there embarrassed for a moment, then started to leave. Before she could get out the door, another man grabbed her hand and whisked her out the back door. "Don't ever be afraid of expressing yourself," he told her. "I think your singing is delightful."

Later that week he called her and they began a long friendship. It was not until two months into this new relationship that she discovered that her rescuer was one of the partners in the firm, and that he had been looking most of his life for a woman who could be spontaneous.

When you fear rejection, it often holds you back from love and happiness. Instead, use it to learn a lesson or lessons and to motivate yourself in new and powerful ways.

People react to fear of rejection in many ways by closing their hearts, feeling sorry for themselves, feeling not good enough, dating people they do not care about, detaching emotionally, avoiding intimacy, and avoiding love.

Remember, do not take rejection personally. Learn from it,

make whatever changes you need to make, and go on. I discovered long ago that the more you love yourself, the less you fear rejection. When you love yourself, you think of rejection as the other person's loss. Bring the fear down to size by asking yourself: What is the worst thing that can happen?

See that disaster happening in your mind. See yourself handling it, then say, "now that wasn't so bad. It probably won't happen but if it does, I'm ready."

Taking More Risks

Taking risks requires faith, courage, and trust which will keep you moving and growing. Herbert Otto, author of *Guide to Developing Your Potential,* said, "Change and growth takes place when a person has risked himself and dares to become involved with experimenting with his own life."

Erich Fromm, author of *The Art of Loving,* also said, "Love is an act of faith and whoever is of little faith is of little love."

According to Leo Buscaglia, our odds are 50 percent. Much better than they are in Las Vegas. "Only the person who risks is truly free."

The more risks you take, the more choices you have. As I was leaving a seminar years ago, I noticed a man inside a circle of five women. They looked like they were having a good time. Instead of leaving, I walked directly over to him and said, "I would like to hug you." He put his arms around me and we left together. After that, we went together for several years.

Let me also give you another example. I had a client named Bill who was a Hollywood movie director. He had divorced his wife a few years before and now decided to take a short vacation home to South Carolina.

The day before he was to return home, he called an old girlfriend, Jeannette, whom he hadn't seen in twenty-five years.

She had also divorced her husband some time back and invited him to come over.

Within a few hours of meeting again, they decided to get back together. She would return with him in two weeks to California. People change in twenty-five years. They had five marriages between them, she had to sell her house, quit her job, and move several thousand miles away without an income.

A risk? Yes, but it worked; they've been together several years and are one of the happiest couples I've ever known.

Think of taking risks as doing new and exciting things. Anything can happen.

Ask yourself: What can I gain by taking the risk? What can I lose? What risks have I taken recently? What risks have I taken recently in my relationships? What happened as a result of taking those risks? What risks would I like to take now? If you have a mate ask him or her to answer as well.

Don't ignore these questions, think about them. They represent a growth opportunity that can lead you on to greater adventures and more complete and fulfilling relationships.

Chapter Twelve

Trust

*I'm very loyal in relationships. Even when I go
out with my mom I don't look at other moms.*
—Gary Shandling

Trusting is being able to rely on your own or another's future behavior. It helps you rise above doubts and negative feelings that a relationship will continue to be a source of fulfillment and joy. Trust brings intimacy, openness, closeness, and connectedness.

To have trust, you must be able to count on the fact that another person will do what he or she agrees to do. I run into what I will call un-trustworthiness sometimes in my work as a counselor. Someone will call and make an appointment, then not show up. I had one client who made three appointments in a row and missed every one of them.

Warren originally came to me to learn how to build more trust and intimacy in his personal and business relationships. He was thirty minutes late, so I called his apartment. His roommate told me where he was. But when he finally called me, he told me that he was somewhere else. This type of behavior breaks down trust.

Being trustworthy means being reliable, dependable, faithful, responsible, credible, believable, constant, true, and loyal. These are necessary qualities to have in any relationship.

I always think of trust in the same terms as I think of the foundation of a house. If that foundation is strong, that house (or that relationship) will be hard to destroy, no matter what anyone else tries to do. If the trust foundation is weak, the relationship is doomed from the beginning.

One of my clients, Eleanor, had been in a relationship for many years and she couldn't trust anything her partner said. If Tim said he was going to work, he probably wasn't. If he said that Friday was payday, it probably meant he had already spent the money. And if he told her he had to work late, it usually meant he was going out with someone else.

When they finally broke up, she was very reluctant to trust anyone else. Her new partner, however, turned out to be as good as his word. If he said he would do something for her, he did it. If he promised to be somewhere at a certain time, he was there. For over a year, she kept waiting for him to slip. He never did.

The last time I saw her she was beaming. "Trust," she told me, "it's wonderful. I'm like a new person. I can tell you, life really is worth living."

You can't trust halfway. You either trust or you do not trust. You can be trusted or you cannot be trusted.

Trusting Yourself

Trusting has a lot to do with liking yourself. If you do not like yourself, it will be hard to believe others will like you. If you do not trust, you will not be trusted.

As a child, Cindy's parents failed to trust her to do anything. As a result, she didn't trust herself either. She didn't trust that she could do any job right. She didn't trust that she could support herself, and she didn't trust her own decisions.

This lack of confidence on Cindy's part extended to everything she did. Others sensed it and became wary of becoming friends with her. At work, other employees and her boss felt that since she didn't believe in herself she probably couldn't be trusted with responsibility either. The result was that Cindy remained alone most of the time and was passed over many times for promotion.

It wasn't until she enrolled in group therapy sessions that she begin to understand how self-trust affects every aspect of life. The result was an immediate improvement of her image, her ability to trust herself, and her acceptance from the outside world.

Trusting yourself allows you to trust others. The more you trust, the more others will trust you.

Emerson said, "Self-trust is the secret of success."

You learned a lot about trusting from your parents. Parents instill trustworthiness in their children by being trustworthy themselves. If a child can trust his or her parents, he or she tends to trust others as well. Parents also help build a child's self-esteem by trusting that child not only to be truthful, but trusting that he or she is capable of performing the tasks assigned. When a parent doesn't trust a child, it undermines that child's confidence and ultimately the child's ability to trust himself or herself.

Now let's try a question-exercise that will help you determine your own level of trust and self-trust.

Ask yourself: What is my history with trust? How does trust show up in my relationships now? What does trusting feel like? What does not trusting feel like? What determines if I will trust someone? Do people have to earn my trust or do I give it automatically? What can I always trust about myself? What do I find difficult to trust about myself? With your partner: What do you trust about me? What do you need to trust more about me? How can we build more trust with each other?

Again, take your time and think it through. Your answers will be enlightening.

Deepening Trust

I personally find that my trust grows in a person when that person shares with me. That is, when I can pour my heart out to someone, and they do the same with me. I have a friend who will listen to my innermost problems but won't share back. I like this friend but the trust and sharing can go just so far. The deeper you get into sharing with your partner, I have found, the more the trust grows, so does the partnership. This particular friendship will remain the same without growing, year after year.

I also find that positive energy builds trust. Think about someone you know who is constantly projecting negative thoughts. They run down other people. They always explain why they can't do something, and they constantly complain. Do you trust them? Of course not. You give your trust to the person who likes people, thinks good thoughts, and can tackle any task.

Finally, I find that I trust someone I can be silly with. This has to do with being accepting and not being judgmental. Suppose, for instance, you've just gotten a promotion and you go to a friend's house. You and your friend do a little dance together, and you treat yourselves to a crazy night on the town. This releasing control and letting down your hair builds trust between you, probably quicker than anything else I can think of.

Not Trusting

Broken trust is difficult to repair. It takes a lot of work to bring trust back and there is no guarantee that the relationship will ever be the same.

For instance, Trudy trusted her husband John explicitly.

During the four years they had been married, John rose quickly in his company. And at the end of the third year, the company sent him on the road as a troubleshooter.

Trudy's trust was so strong that she thought nothing of his being away from home a week or two at a time.

One evening, however, she phoned his hotel room to tell him that his mother was coming to stay with them that weekend. Much to her chagrin, a woman answered. Ordinarily, she would have been positive she had the wrong number, but she could hear John in the background. When he came on the phone, he stuttered and stammered and finally confessed everything.

Trudy was devastated. After thinking about it for a long time she decided to stay with John. Together, they worked on their marriage very hard in couples counseling for over a year. But even today the relationship is not the same, and as far as Judy is concerned, it never will be.

A lack of trust means you will never be sure of what you mean to another person. No matter what they tell you, you will not believe them totally.

Without trust you will hold back your feelings because you will keep your guard up and distance yourself. You will not feel free to be yourself.

Not trusting will cause you to worry about being hurt because you will not be able to count on your partner to be there for you. You will be pulled apart.

Let's do another one of our quick surveys. Ask yourself: What effect has trusting had on my relationships? What effect has a lack of trust had on them? The answers to these two questions will help you understand why lack of trust can be a problem and help you understand and use trust as a relationship tool.

Building Trust

To build trust you must be willing to take the risk of trusting. Here are some ways to build it:

• Let yourself be vulnerable to another person. Simply take the risk of being hurt. The more positive reinforcement you receive the stronger your trust becomes.
• Overcome your fears. This can be a hard one. And it is almost like letting yourself be vulnerable. If, for instance, you fear that by trusting you will lose someone, you must do it anyway. Again, the more positive reinforcement you receive the stronger you become.
• Be honest. Honesty creates honesty in another person.
• Be sensitive. Understand that a partner will make mistakes or that there will be misunderstandings.
• Give your partner room to grow. Trusting someone doesn't mean checking on them, or holding them tightly. It means letting go.
• Keep your thoughts positive. Positive thoughts create their own energy, and help build trust in the process.
• Acknowledge your partner. Trust your partner, and at times let them know that you appreciate trustworthiness.
• Stop cynical thoughts. How easy it is to be cynical. Especially after you've been in a relationship where you couldn't trust the other person at all. It's easy to say, "I can't trust anyone." Stop! Give your partner the benefit of the doubt until he or she proves you wrong.
• Be silly with your partner. This is another way of saying "let your hair down," and encourage your partner do the same. It gives you a chance to see and share a part of you, you never could any other way.

• Take risks. As we saw in the last chapter, taking risks with a partner increases intimacy and trust.

• Keep all agreements with yourself and others. This is all important. Other people must be able to trust that you will do what you say you will.

• Share and reveal yourself. Again, this gives your partner a deeper insight into your personality and builds lasting trust.

Chapter Thirteen

Intimacy

*Intimacy is like reading a terrific book. When you
open it you can really enjoy yourself.*
—Susan Scott

Intimacy brings wealth to the riches of love. It brings much
pleasure, closeness, warmth, and sharing. It brings out the best
in you when you are in an ideal relationship.

Arthur Deikman, author of *Personal Freedom,* described
intimacy as "the feeling of not having to be guarded with
another person. This requires trust, positive evaluation of self,
and acceptance of our own thoughts, feelings, and impulses."

My definition of intimacy is understanding and being who
you are with someone else who understands and is being who
they are. Both partners have to be real, which means they are
telling the truth, taking risks, and sharing all feelings. They are
vulnerable and show their flaws and insecurities.

Let's look at an example of this. Both Bill and Cindy had
relationships in the past where their partners wouldn't reveal
themselves in any way. After Bill terminated the relationship,
he discovered his partner had been married several times before
and really didn't like doing any of the activities they par-
ticipated in together. She hadn't shared this with him. Cindy, on
the other hand, discovered that her partner had a police record

and was wanted in several states. He hadn't shared this either.

When they began their relationship, Cindy shared that she had given birth to a child out of wedlock and turned him over to another couple for adoption. Bill shared that he had just been fired from his job as a middle manager and was feeling angry and depressed.

While these revelations might have caused either partner to terminate the relationship, they didn't. In fact, the problems that troubled each person helped bring them closer together.

Sharing intimacy is loving each other for who you are in unconditional ways. "Be yourself. No one can ever tell you you're doing it wrong," said James Leo Herling.

As you see the beauty in yourself, you will see it in others.

You will be the happiest and grow the most when you have the most intimate relationship. It is when you stop sharing that love fades.

The alternatives to intimacy are superficial love and loneliness.

"Intimacy is a road, not a goal." It's an on-going process, as alive as the two people are who create and live it.

Fear of Intimacy

While many people long for intimacy, many fear it at the same time. It is frightening to those who do not want to know themselves or to be known to others. Revealing who they are, even to themselves, often seems overwhelming.

Let me share an example. Louise, a schoolteacher at a San Francisco elementary school, seemed terrified at revealing anything about herself to other people. I learned that Louise projected herself as a terrific teacher and someone who was much in demand as a speaker in educational circles. She constantly announced this to anyone who would listen.

The truth was, I learned from others, that Louise was always in trouble with the administration. Her students hated her. She just barely got out of college. She had to repeat her student teaching twice, and she had never given a speech to anyone.

She had built the image of herself that she wanted to project, and was terrified to reveal who she really was. In truth, Louise could be a charming and wonderful person . . . but because she tried to hide who she was, very few people would ever know the real Louise.

Those who fear opening up to themselves and others know they have to take risks, possibly experience hurt and pain, have demands made on them, make changes, and reveal their deepest feelings.

Most people who fear intimacy also feel they take the risk of boring others . . . of not being liked . . . of becoming jealous . . . of not wanting to take on another's problems . . . of not wanting to be dependent on anyone else or anyone else being dependent on them . . . of being used . . . of losing control . . . of being rejected or abandoned . . . and of getting stuck with the wrong partner.

The end result most of us fear is pain. The truth is that without intimacy we won't have love, closeness, or sharing. And this will eventually create pain, despair, and loneliness, and relationships that fail to grow.

Imagine watching a sad movie and not feeling anything. Imagine watching a happy movie and not feeling anything. I have found that the degree in which you feel pain is in direct proportion to the degree in which you feel joy and love. Love is a packaged deal filled with both joy and sorrow.

Let me share with you, from my workshops, some of the characteristics I have observed in those who fear intimacy. They are often erratic, selfish, object oriented, undependable, have a lack of commitment, fail to accept themselves, attempt to be totally perfect or totally bad, and lead with their heads rather than their hearts.

Destroying Intimacy

We have seen that fears destroy intimacy. But, many other things do, too. Here's a list: having affairs, lying, money problems, breaking agreements, a lack of quality time, exaggerated expectations, subjugating self and personal power, trying to change a partner, and indifference.

Nick, a banker acquaintance of mine, managed to use each one of them. In the course of his many relationships, I have seen him lie to his partner, cheat on her, stay away days at a time when he promised to take her somewhere, and simply ignore the other person's needs. It's no wonder he never could keep a relationship for more than a few weeks at a time. Intimacy is a powerful tool in a relationship, but it's also a fragile one that can easily be destroyed by a lack of personal integrity.

Neediness

If you crave someone else, you probably also crave yourself.

You are attracted to that which you need to complete yourself. Plato's theory of love was, "the longing for completion is longing to meld with another person." I define neediness as an unfulfilled desire for affection and love. Sometimes it becomes an uncontrolled drive. "Needy" people often go out "looking" for love. They continually look for someone to love them or to give them attention. You see them frequently in singles bars and elsewhere. Their eyes search out the possibilities wherever they go. Unfortunately, the only people they will attract are needy people.

Melanie, a client, wanted a relationship so badly that she agreed to marry Russ even though he was untrustworthy and a manic depressive. She was so hungry for attention that she swept aside all possible problems. Her parents died when she was a little girl leaving her hungry for love and affection.

Before Melanie got rid of Russ, he had taken her home away, and swindled her out of sixty thousand dollars. Everyone else could have predicted the impending disaster, but Melanie wouldn't listen. Her need for love was too great.

Let me give you another example. Millie and Arthur were on their first two-week vacation since being married five years ago. Arthur was in another room, watching movies, alone.

The longer Millie waited for him to come to bed, the more irritated she became at his lack of attention. When her hurt feelings built to a crescendo, she blurted out, "You don't really want to be with me!" The fight that followed could be heard clear to the motel office.

To resolve this situation peacefully, Millie could have 1) communicated her feelings and offered constructive solutions that met both of their needs; 2) gone into the next room and watched the movie with Arthur; 3) decided to enjoy the vacation rather than dwell on the negative; 4) loved Arthur unconditionally and recognized that he needed some time and space to be alone.

Needing attention means being "needy" for love. However, looking outside yourself for love is rarely satisfying. You can really only find love and contentment within yourself.

If you have this problem, I have a solution. Visualize opening your heart. Visualize filling it with your self. See yourself as complete and satisfied. See yourself enjoying being alone, and knowing that you are complete within yourself. You will soon discover that you can fill your own heart with your own love and need not seek love from others. Fortunately, when you fill your own heart you then attract others to love at the same time.

Practicing Intimacy

Here is an exercise I use in my workshops I think you will find helpful. I suggest to everyone that they practice intimacy every chance they get. Practice relating to and talking to people on elevators, in grocery stores, everywhere. Ask them any simple question, such as "what is the most interesting thing that has happened to you today?" You'll be surprised at some of the conversations you will have. I always find, too, that the mailman is a good person to practice on because he has to come back every day!

Let me also let you in on a secret that we talked about in this chapter. When you share feelings with someone they generally open up much faster than when you simply say, "hello." Just for practice, with a friend or your relationship partner, try sharing some of the following feelings. Try one of you going down the entire list first and then switch to the other person. Look into each other's eyes while doing this process. Ask: What makes you feel excited, lonely, angry, interested, confident, insecure, resistant, nervous, ashamed, special, fulfilled, motivated, ashamed, spiteful, calm, aloof, secure, insecure, destructive, inhibited, emotional, carefree, cynical, pessimistic, optimistic, quiet, envious, proud, passionate, responsible, irresponsible, obstinate, stubborn, depressed, impressed, sensitive, cautious, envious, thoughtful, embarrassed, selfish, loose, uptight, comfortable, possessive, generous, humble, inhibited, shy, bored, elated, hurt, worried, obsessed, vulnerable, guilty, weak, strong, and flexible? Also try sharing what makes you laugh and what makes you sad. Just pick one or two and work some conversation about it. Ask others in your life to share their feelings, too.

Here's a sample. "I've just seen something that makes me extremely sad. . . ." "Let me tell you about something funny I just saw." Just use your imagination and do the best you can. You'll be very surprised at what happens.

Good relationships aren't created by accident or because your number was called. You can't go into Macy's and buy a relationship kit. If you want a deep and intimate relationship, you must first understand what goes into making a growing, healthy relationship, then you must learn to create those basics in your own life. Intimacy is a vital essential, without which no real relationship can exist.

Increasing Intimacy

Here are some pointers I have found useful. Try them and see which work best for you.

- Love and care about yourself. Taking care of yourself always helps increase intimacy with others.
- Be open and honest. Honesty implies intimacy. It says you can be trusted.
- Risk rejection. Putting yourself at risk with another person always helps bring you closer to that person.
- Show how much you care. Caring always calls for an emotional reaction on the part of the other person.
- Accept your partner without judgments. Acceptance knocks down barriers that rejection throws up.
- Be available for the other person. Availability helps another person know that you accept them. Not being available makes that individual pull back.
- Be supportive. Everyone needs and wants support. The more unconditional that support the better.
- Be a good friend. Being a good friend means being open and upfront with the other person. It always means going the extra mile.

• Give and receive feedback. Good give-and-take always helps increase understanding and closeness.

• Make eye contact. Eye contact says "I'm interested in you."

• Listen well. Listening helps show the other person that you care and that you want to know what they are saying. Listening always creates an intimate response.

• Spend quality time alone. This enforces your own feeling of self-sufficiency, and helps others feel comfortable with you.

• Spend quality time together. Have special times planned for only each other.

• Plan the future. When you plan with another person it says, I want to be with you.

• Share fantasies. Fantasies help create a world that only the two of you share.

• Be in present time. As much as you might like to talk of the past, it generally throws up a roadblock to intimacy. Unless you are talking about something you did together in the past, stay in the here and now.

• Give yourself totally without holding back. The other person will sense that you are giving your all and will respond.

• Keep agreements. Not keeping agreements breaks trust and throws up intimacy roadblocks.

• Grow together. Every good relationship requires growth. The more you create common interests, the more intimacy you create.

• Create common goals. Shared goals invite two people to work and grow together.

• Express yourself fully. By all means be as candid as possible and share your innermost thoughts.

• Laugh and play. Laughing and playing opens up emotional communication and promotes intimacy.

• Sing and dance. Like laughing and playing, singing and dancing helps create an emotional bond.

- Travel together. Travel builds shared experiences and creates common goals.
- Make love.
- Surrender to what is. Accepting things as they are helps create a "we're-in-this-together atmosphere."
- Bond spiritually.
- Do creative projects together. These create much the same spirit as fun and singing and dancing.

Now, I want to give you a series of questions to answer. They will help you determine where you are right now.

What does intimacy mean to me? What are my fears of intimacy? What do I like about intimacy? What do I dislike? What has destroyed my intimate relationships? What has blocked intimacy in my relationships? What are the differences between intimacy as I experience it now and as I would like it to be? Whom have I felt intimate with in the past? Whom do I feel intimate with now? What do I need to do to achieve more intimacy?

Again, take your time. It doesn't hurt to ask and answer these questions several times alone and with your relationship partner if you are in a couple. If you decide intimacy is one of your problems, I suggest you reread this chapter, and try the exercises again.

Chapter Fourteen

Sexuality

The process of sex is the pattern of all the process of our life.
—Havelock Ellis, author of *The New Spirit*

Because people love good sex, sex is powerful! Sex is often mistaken for love, but sex is not love. Love is not crucial to sex.

Erich Fromm said in *The Art of Loving,* "It seems that sexual desire can easily blend with and be stimulated by love."

There are two kinds of sex. One is a physical merging and the other is an expression of loving. The latter includes intimacy, spirituality, giving, and receiving.

Stewart Emery, founder of Actualizations, says, "Sex is two people coming together to play. The trouble is, they bring their minds with them." Sexuality is part of your heart and is not controlled by your mind. Your heart center is your love center and when you cry out for sex you are crying out for love.

Because sex can become addictive, the ongoing need for love can become even stronger as long as the addiction continues. I have seen many people filled with such high sexual energy that they project it onto anyone they relate with, whether they are attracted to them or not. Sex addicts usually end up attracting mostly physical merging, but continue to long for love as they experience loneliness and disappointment.

For instance, Jerome, a computer engineer, filled his work-day with thoughts of sex. As a result he literally radiated animal magnetism. Even though he never said anything suggestive, the women in the office always had the feeling that he wanted to have sex with them.

As one of them said, "He's really a nice guy, but I'll never go out with him because I'd feel like a sex object."

As a result, Jerome had lots of one-night stands, but he was never able to communicate on a deeper level. And although I know he really wants a deeper commitment, I am sure he'll never create one, until he integrates his sexuality into his entire personality.

Actress Jean Harlow said, "My God, must I always wear a low-cut dress to be important?"

While sex does not produce love, it has been used to get many different things: a relationship, a date, an adventure, attention, an ego boost, relief of sexual urge, and exercise. Sex has also been used to prove one's self-worth . . . to obtain acceptance . . . to attempt to feel closer to someone . . . to patch up arguments . . . to create amusement and fun, and to stimulate curiosity.

Choosing Your Sexuality

You choose the meaning of your sexuality and the role it plays in your life. Both the meaning and the role keep changing as you change. There will be times you will feel very sexual and times you will not feel sexual at all. Freud said, "Human beings are not by nature sexual, but they choose to be."

Many of your sexual decisions are based on and influenced by a host of situations in life concerning stress, body weight, career, money, and health.

Sex plays many different and interesting roles in our lives and in our relationships. Elvis Presley was known for having slept with one thousand women before marrying Priscilla. He usually videotaped his sex. Because he was insecure, he liked young and inexperienced girls so he would not be rejected or compared to other men.

Charlie Chaplain was called, "a human sex machine" because he was good for six "bouts" with only five minutes in between. He was known to be a voyeur and had a telescope that looked into John Barrymore's bedroom.

Picasso said, "For me, there are only two kinds of women—goddesses and doormats!"

Think about the sexual choices you are making and know that you can make new choices anytime. Sex and sexuality will be what you want them to be.

Barbara, a pleasant woman client, wanted sex to be a giving of herself completely to someone, and to have that person give completely to her. In the beginning she kept creating partners who wanted sex for sex's sake, but as she began to learn who she was, she was able to open herself up to others, and her partners returned the feeling. The last time I saw Barbara she was extremely happy with a single partner, who she said, filled her every need.

You can choose to bring your sexual energy up or down. You can bring it up with your thoughts and fantasies, and down with food, negative thoughts, and emotional feelings such as anger.

Not only do you choose when and how to have sex with someone, but you choose when you want to talk about it.

Mensa, a group of people with exceptionally high IQs, invited me to give a lecture about commitment. Instead of dealing with the topic, they kept switching their focus to sex so much, that I had to change the topic to sex.

Some think you have to choose between sexuality and spirituality. They are connected, not separate issues. A well-known founder of the human potential movement thought because he chose to become a spiritual leader that he should not have sexual feelings.

While conducting a workshop, he became upset when someone questioned him about relationships. He finally asked the group not to talk about that subject. When they persisted, he became angry. And the angrier he became, the more they persisted. Obviously, they were asking the wrong teacher.

I discovered long ago, you get what you want sexually when you choose what you want!

Ask yourself: How much importance do I attribute to my sexuality? Does the importance of sex differ when I am not in love? What sexual choices am I making? How do I choose when to have sex with someone? How has the meaning of sex changed for me in the past year? The answers to these questions will help you determine your overall sexual attitudes.

Definitions of Sex

In my workshops, each participant is asked to write down his or her own definition of sexuality. Each person's definition is truly personal and unique. After seeing hundreds of personal interpretations I have never seen two that were alike.

I always ask workshop participants to define sexuality. I want to share them with you here.

• Being with a person you love and being able to love the person.
• How you are looked upon by others, how good you feel with someone and or by yourself.
• To have sex.
• The physical expression of a loving relationship in which male and female energy expresses the dynamics.
• The way you respond to, and elicit from others, sexual feelings.

- The way a person looks and expresses themselves.
- Someone who makes my blood hot.
- The creative life-force.
- Communicating through your body.
- Having your needs fulfilled to capacity.
- Allowing the other person to express his real needs and letting him share his fantasies—as well as allowing me to express my needs.
- The ultimate intimate sharing of a highlighted closeness which fulfills each other's personal expectations resulting in a satisfying state of common resolution.
- Unification of spirit.
- Being wanted and exciting someone.
- Feeling the ecstasy of the complete union of two people as one.
- Being able to express love and intimacy without words.
- The ability to act out or put into expression your true inner self.
- Knowing your attraction to the opposite gender and expressing that attraction and fulfilling your needs.
- To be totally available to a person who will accept it.
- Giving myself 100 percent.
- How my sexual desire causes me to behave.
- The ability to convey your inner strength and love, your vulnerability and inner power with honestly and unconditionally sharing.
- Feeling beautiful all over.
- The physical expression of love and mutual attraction through unrestricted passionate embraces, touching, and deep energetic contact.
- Bonding, oneness and toe curling.
- A good screw with lust, potent energy, and melting.
- Genital-related thoughts of contact.
- Being responsive to someone and aware of your own needs.

• When I accept and love myself as a sexual person.

• An all encompassing aura of self-expression that reveals the innermost qualities of one's life at any point in time.

• When I feel warm all over from being with the right woman.

• Awareness and appreciation of the body as a tool for physical enjoyment.

• An expression of "being" in the body concerning relationships.

• Giving and receiving physical pleasure and merging energies.

• Ability to screw my lover's brains out!

• Interest in having a sexual relationship.

• Enjoying coming together.

• When two people look at each other and meet and flow together.

• Being totally free to express your desires and totally free to receive your male's desires.

• The way a person moves, dresses, speaks, and touches you.

• The ability to excite another person by openly expressing what one desires to achieve the ultimate pleasure.

• Accepting the blessings of being able to express your sexual self fully with your partner and focusing on using that part of you to fulfill your partner.

• The giving of oneself in a total fulfilling physical way and peaking to ultimate release and exhaustion.

• The way you feel in your body about your body.

• Flirting and foreplay, time for love and sometimes quickies.

• Making heavenly love with another through the body, mind, and spirit.

• My inner glow and sense of self, vibrantly expressed verbally, physically, mentally, and emotionally.

• Animal magnetism and charisma.

- The joyful and triumphant surge of loving consciousness in action.
- To be three feet off the floor.
- Sharing life with another person and recreating at-one-ment.
- Desire to please and receive pleasure physically from someone you love.
- Satisfaction of physical desire for two separate bodies to become one being.
- Baring your wants, needs and desires.
- Feeling attractive.
- Being uninhibited and nonjudgmental of each other's turn-on.
- Being myself and sharing that with another person and with love and joy.
- Accepting being a male or female and experiencing without blocks the pros and cons of sex.
- The physical and emotional sensations that create sexual excitement.
- The ability to give and receive pleasure.
- A spontaneous joyous-love connection.
- The highest form of spiritual connection.
- The creative expression of desire, be it spiritual, mental and/or physical desire. No, make it 80 percent physical desire.
- The situation where you remain physically excited with your partner over a long time period, even though their body isn't as pretty as a centerfold.
- Physical vehicle to life's greatest experience.
- A chemistry between two people that is indescribably passionate and all-consuming.
- The essence of beings.
- Turning you on.
- Loving someone's touch.
- How I present my masculinity to other people.

• The expression of a person's maleness or femaleness in action and words.

• Fun sharing of passionate core, sweet, nasty, and full of heat and magic.

• Being comfortable with the other sex.

• All forms of enjoying bodies.

• Not having anything to hide.

• The physical manifestation of the spiritual union of the male and female aspects of God, where my partner and I are experiencing God in each other.

• Feeling power and strength over other people, feeling masterful and in charge.

• The way in which a person relates to themself and the world based on their feelings and perceptions of their own body.

• Super fantastic highly desirable sense of self.

• Erotic motion, flirtatious eye contact, directed nudity, and showing ass.

• Being with another person in ways that make you both sexually aroused.

• The awareness of sexual needs and pleasures and how they relate to a positive relationship with sensitivity.

• Erotic sensuality.

• Being able to perform mentally and physically.

• The ability to find oneself attractive and share that with others.

• The desire of and experience of physical closeness.

• The sharing of intercourse with another human.

• An investigation of the sensory-motor process by way of the heart, mind, and body, usually but not always involving genitalia.

• Being open and alert to physical stimuli of many different kinds.

• A relationship combining people's animalistic natures to their intellectual capacities.

- The magic of arousal and excitement that connects the body with the mind and the subconscious with the conscious.
- Your unique method of verbal and nonverbal seduction.
- Being in tune with someone else.
- Wanting to do anything and everything and getting it back.
- Being safe and completely and mutually adored.

While each person's definition of sexuality differs, you are affected mentally, physically, emotionally, and spiritually by sex. Not only does sexuality mean something different to each of you, it tells a lot about you.

Ask yourself: What does sexuality mean to me? What does sexuality mean to my partner? What is my sexual self-image? These answers will begin to define your sexuality at the moment and will tell you whether you have learned the lesson put forth in this chapter or need to work on it.

Sexual Problems

Any sexual problems you have are actually relationship problems that are manifested through sexuality. They could be fear of intimacy, fear of rejection, fear of risking, unresolved anger and resentment, lack of self-confidence, inability to receive pleasure from another, and communication and deprivation. A strong aversion to a sexual act may be due to anger with that person. And fear of any aspect of sex may be due to an inability to trust.

Ernest Hemingway had a limited sexual capacity. He believed that each man was alloted a certain number of orgasms in his life and that these had to be carefully spaced out!

Howard Hughes developed a problem when his dog bit him in his penis which required six stitches!

Betty Bethards, author and psychic, said, "If you're stuffing

your sexuality, you'll have a lot of problems." When you feel
unfulfilled in sex, you will try to compensate in other areas of
your life or have a preoccupation with sexual ideas. Have you
ever heard someone who is continually telling bad sexual jokes?

Paul, for instance, experimented briefly with sex as a teen-
ager, but he was clumsy and inept with the two girls he at-
tempted to go to bed with. As a result they ridiculed him and
would never go out with him again. This turned Paul off to sex
from then on. As an adult he became a workaholic. He seldom
dated, and spent most of his time at the office working on pet
projects. He rose rapidly in the firm, but his life was miserable.
When I first met Paul, I found him to be extremely unhappy. He
asked: "Will I ever be able to have sex again?" Actually, the
solution was easy. Paul simply needed to create a woman who
liked him for himself and one who was willing to be patient.
Once he realized this, he soon found a woman who thought he
was the greatest thing in the world. The last time I saw him, he
announced proudly that he was getting married.

While sex is one of the most difficult issues for couples to
communicate about, sexual problems are easy to correct. As you
have seen with Paul you simply need to understand what the
real trouble is and do something about it.

Sometimes you only need to make a few adjustments. Here
are some of the changes that I often find need to be made: Create
an ideal or appropriate partner . . . Change the environment . . .
Create a different atmosphere . . . Learn new techniques and
positions . . . Deal with feelings and emotions . . . Communicate
more openly . . . Add romance . . . and Balance the giving and
receiving.

Sex is a natural urge, necessary for growth and development, and can bring a sense of happiness.

Ask yourself: What is missing from my sexuality? How can
I add it to my life? How do I stuff my sexuality? If I do, why do
I? What are my negative thoughts about my sexuality? How has

what my parents taught me about sex affected my sex life? What do I dislike about sex?

Again, these are not questions to be read and not answered. Answer them, then think about them and try to draw some conclusions as to how sex affects your life right now.

Communication and Sex

Some people are afraid to communicate their sexual needs and problems because of the following reasons: They are embarrassed; they fear hurting or offending their partner; they will ruin the spontaneity of the moment; or they fear they are being selfish.

You need to communicate to express yourself and to create a more satisfying sex life. Not expressing a feeling or a need will cause that feeling to build up. Feelings that build up become resentments and anger. Anger prevents you from responding sexually. Communicating transforms sex in positive ways.

I see this many times in my practice. Gerald and his wife Irene had been married ten years. When they were first married, Irene frequently initiated sex. But the last three years, he waited for her to make the next move and she never did. As a result, he became frustrated and more irritated. By the time he said something to Irene he was almost ready to explode.

It turned out that she had pulled back because she thought she was being too aggressive and that he didn't really like it. The truth was they both misunderstood. Once they had communicated their feelings, however, Irene returned being sexually aggressive and Bob loved it. This problem, like many other sexual problems, was solved through good clear communication.

To use communication in positive ways:

- Be specific about what you want and do not want.
- Ask questions.

- Express all feelings.
- Communicate before, during, and after sex.
- Acknowledge your partner.
- Respond to your partner's needs.

Ask yourself: What am I afraid to communicate about? What am I afraid to ask for sexually?

Touching

How much you like to touch and be touched is an influence on your sexuality. The more you like someone, the more you will touch them. Touching is the most intense of the senses and is what you remember the most in past relationships.

You need to be touched. Infants who are not fondled die. Freud said, "The base of all mental illness is the lack of sensual gratification." (Freud was labeled a "dirty old man.")

While touching is enjoyable and healing, some are afraid to touch.

Creating Ideal Sex

Sex involves all the senses, most mental energies, and all parts of the body. Physiologically, men and women are more similar than they are different. The more natural you are about sex, the more creative you will be. The more creative you are, the more dimensions of sex will unfold for you. It is all up to the participants to create good sex.

The longer you prolong having sex with someone new, the better chances of a longer-lasting relationship. Take the time to build an intimate bond, trust, and good communication with each other first.

Your feelings within yourself and your thoughts, words, and

actions create your sexual reality. You get what you want sexually when you become who you are.

Pointers for creating ideal sex:

- Show your partner how magnificent they are and experience them as magnificent.
- You are responsible for the receiving of sexuality.
- Talking about sex will bring on sexual energy.
- Know what turns you on and what turns your partner on.
- Make agreements with your partner.
- Do not make assumptions.
- Understand each other's commitment.
- Find out each other's expectations from sex (being playful, purely physical, deeply spiritual, passion, and excitement).
- Keep a sexual journal.
- Know each other's physical, emotional, and spiritual needs.
- Be playful.
- Share fantasies.
- Set the stage with candles, lighting, incense, flowers, and music.
- Write a script of what your ideal sexual scene would be like. Describe your partner. How would you respond to each other? How would you feel? Where are you, what time of day, for how long, how often, and what is the mood like?
- Trade off times of giving each other pleasure.
- Keep your hearts open and connected to each other.

Sex will be what you want it to be.

Ask yourself and your partner: What brings out my sexuality? What negative thoughts do I have to change about my sexuality? What do I like about sex? What turns me on? What are my sexual needs? What is sexy about me?

Chapter Fifteen

Jealousy

Yet he was jealous, though he did not show it,
For jealousy dislike the world to know it.
—Lord Byron

Jealousy is a natural response, an instinctive reaction to certain types of threats in a relationship. Jealousy starts during infancy and early childhood when most of us learn basic survival needs. As you mature, jealousy becomes a learned reaction which helps protect love and relationships when they appear to be threatened.

People react out of jealousy when the following appear jeopardized: love . . . your feeling of attractiveness . . . your partner's commitment . . . control . . . loss of face . . . the quality of the relationship . . . your home . . . happiness . . . affection . . . pride . . . status . . . your future . . . privacy . . . sexual/intellectual/emotional needs . . . time with your partner.

Partners also often trigger jealousy by exaggerating the appeal of a third person, flirting with others, dating others, talking about previous partners, and sometimes even paying attention to the children.

To see how this works, let's look at a number of examples:

• A former client, Sandra, ordinarily wasn't jealous of anyone. But after she married Phil, a handsome attorney, she sometimes felt twinges of jealousy when beautiful women gathered around him at parties.

Usually, she just ignored the feelings, but when she discovered he had taken one of the office secretaries home without her knowledge, her whole life flashed before her eyes.

"I could," she said, "see myself losing my home, my husband, and in effect my whole life. I did something about it, however. I talked to my husband immediately.

He seemed surprised and concerned by my feelings. It was the best thing I ever did, because, since then, he's gone out of his way to make sure I have nothing to worry about."

• When Laura and Billy started living together five years ago, Billy found himself becoming jealous of Laura's five-year-old daughter Cindy. Billy was macho, and obsessed with his body and physical image. In his mind, Cindy represented someone who took up too much of Laura's time. As a result, he began to physically and emotionally abuse the child. Laura was so needy for a relationship, that she sent Cindy to live with her father. The father soon moved the child to the Midwest, a thousand miles from Laura, and not long after that the couple broke up. The result was that Laura lost both her relationship and her child.

• Ray, an investment banker, was faithful, honest, and always communicated in positive and loving ways. Yet Lyla was constantly jealous. Ray offered a ride to a female neighbor, Lyla threw a fit. This put Ray in a difficult situation. If he withdrew his offer to the neighbor, he lost respect in his own eyes, the neighbor's eyes, and ultimately in Lyla's eyes.

As a result, he refused to tell the neighbor she couldn't ride with him. When Lyla realized he wouldn't back down, she stalked out of the house and never came back. "I regret losing her," Ray told me, "but until she overcomes her jealousy, she'll never be able to live with anybody."

• On a weekend camping trip, with her husband Larry, Sarah discovered a book in the bottom of one of the duffel bags that she hadn't seen before. When she thumbed through it, a letter written by another woman fell out. Sarah picked it up, read it, and discovered her husband was having an affair. He denied it. And this started a fight which ended with Sarah stalking off into the woods.

Back home that night, Sarah started drinking and wound up phoning "the other woman's" husband. The end result was that Sarah's jealousy broke up two homes. When Sarah had time to think about her actions, she decided that she should have pre-planned what she would do in this situation. "The results for my marriage," she told me, "wouldn't have been any different, because I wouldn't put up with that kind of behavior in a partner, but I certainly could have acted in a more controlled and logical manner."

• Finally, Lisa, one of my workshop participants, became jealous of Dan's old girlfriend Reena because he always spoke so highly of her. Lisa was insecure and when Dan mentioned that he had been unfaithful to other partners in the past, Lisa's insecurities mounted.

One day just as the two of them were feeling very romantic and were about to go to bed, the old girlfriend called to talk. Instead of being sensitive to Lisa, Dan continued talking on and on. Finally, Lisa couldn't stand it another moment and yanked the phone out of Dan's hand and hung up.

This created a tense situation that could have been handled beforehand. Lisa could have told Dan she was jealous, and asked that he recognize this when he talked to Reena in front of her. And/or Dan could have avoided a prolonged conversation with an old girlfriend, since he knew Lisa was insecure. A little sensitivity here would have gone a long ways.

Society's Message

Society often sends the message that jealousy is bad, uncool, an embarrassment, unacceptable, not normal, and that you are not okay if you experience it. That's why it is often called the green-eyed monster.

Some people confirm jealousy, others deny it exists. Jealousy is natural and normal and can serve a relationship in positive ways if you understand the role it plays.

In the beginning of my relationship with my husband, I sometimes found myself becoming jealous. Women would often come up and flirt with him right in front of me. He seemed to not notice. Once I explained that I felt hurt that he did nothing to stop the situation, and taught him to be aware of the women's actions, this never occurred again.

Other people can be very envious of couples who are newly in love and sometimes try to just stir things up for the couple without really wanting anything from the person they are coming on to. These people are troublemakers in general. It is important to have integrity and not flirt with someone else's partner.

The real problem is not jealousy, but how you handle and deal with it. Listen to your jealousy. It's natural and it may give you an early warning that you won't receive any other way.

Jealously is always a signal to take a look at your relationship and often has to do with trust. You might not trust because you don't trust yourself. You have an inner insecurity or you feel there is some relationship problem. If you feel jealous, it is time to pay attention to how satisfying the relationship is and to look at the existing level of trust. If the problem lies within yourself, work on it. If it lies within the relationship, learn the lesson and move on.

Descartes said, "Jealousy is a kind of fear, related to preserve a possession." Sokoloff said, "Jealousy is the least known of all human emotions, the least spoken of human reactions."

Jealousy is usually uncomfortable for those who experience it, whether it is real or imagined. It can easily take over your thoughts, emotions, and actions.

Some of the many emotions and feelings jealousy evokes are: anger, hatred, shame, grief, betrayal, anxiety, humility, sorrow, suspicion, fear, helplessness, insecurity, being left out, unappreciated, guilt, self-righteousness, loneliness, and not feeling good enough.

The Experience Difference

Different people experience jealously in different ways. Your understanding of love and relationships shapes how you will understand and feel about jealousy. In addition, jealous feelings change over time just the way love changes.

For example, Janet tells me that when her partner spends extra time working in his home office, she always feels pangs of jealousy. She reacts to this by constantly raiding the refrigerator during his evening work hours.

Neil, on the other hand, reacts in a completely different way. He loves the attention that men pay to his beautiful wife Diane as long as it's not too much attention. After one individual monopolized her time for over fifteen minutes, he began to fidget. After half an hour, he found himself pacing up and down. "I've tried to break myself of the habit," he told his friends, "but I can't seem to help it."

And in a final example, Leah hates it when her husband of seven years talks to his mother on the phone. Andrew's mother lives in another city and he calls her once a week. "It's an irrational jealousy," she says, "but I don't want to share one minute of his time."

The people who do not admit to being jealous are either not being honest with themselves or with their partners. Jealousy is experienced by everyone at certain times.

Ask yourself: When I am jealous what is being threatened? What am I afraid of? What feelings and emotions do I experience?

Facts About Jealousy

Jealousy has to do with your insecurity level. Jealousy is a threat to your self-esteem. It feeds on itself. The more jealous you are, the more insecure you become. The more insecure you become, the more jealous you are. If you feel incomplete without your mate, the more susceptible you will be.

Conversely, the more secure you are in a relationship, the less jealous you will be. Jealously tends to surface in the beginning stages of relationships, so the longer you are in a relationship, the more secure you feel. Research also shows that younger people are generally more jealous than older ones. Men try to deny jealousy more often than women do. And even animals show insecurity and jealousy.

Positive Elements of Jealousy

Jealousy can serve you in many positive ways:

- It can bring renewed sexual interest to the relationship.
- It can reenforce your feelings towards each other.
- It prevents taking the relationship and each other for granted.
- It provides a chance to reevaluate the relationship.
- It reaffirms the commitment in the relationship.

- It provides an opportunity to make the relationship stronger.
- It can help get more of your needs met.

If you recognize the valuable lessons that jealousy provides, you will grow as you learn. Jealousy signals you to take new actions.

Ask yourself: What have I learned as a result of jealousy? How have my relationships grown through jealousy? How have I reacted to jealousy? How would I handle an unfaithful mate? How do I see myself when I am jealous? If my partner does not get jealous, do I react by thinking he or she doesn't care? How do I feel when someone becomes jealous of me? Have I ever tried to get a partner jealous on purpose? Can I admit jealous feelings?

As before, let these answers be your guide to future actions.

Handling Jealousy

There are seven general ways to deal with jealousy:

1. You can leave the relationship. Unfortunately, all issues of insecurity, trust, and jealousy will come up again in the next relationship.

2. You can get even and have an affair. This seldom provides a real answer, and frequently marks the end of the relationship.

3. You can hit your partner. Only kidding.

4. You can deny it.

5. You can accept the relationship just as it is without doing anything.

6. You can reduce your commitment to the relationship.

7. You can improve the relationship. This requires that both partners communicate honestly about the past, present and future.

You have to find solutions that work for both of you, and you have to make agreements about what each will do when jealousy occurs. Test these agreements and make the necessary changes in them. If you are committed to handle jealousy as a way to grow and improve your connections, you will become closer and more bonded with one another.

For instance, my clients Harry and Mollie had been happily engaged six months when they attended Harry's company Christmas party. They were content, radiant, and had a love-glow around them. A female coworker joined them, pushed herself against Harry, and started making advances. He ignored the coworker's advances while Mollie remained courteous but shocked and pained inside.

On their way home, Mollie expressed her anger and hurt. Harry claimed he didn't know what was happening. Mollie, however, insisted that he do something to stop his coworker's advances.

Finally, they agreed that whenever either of them felt threatened or insecure, that person would step on the partner's foot so they would become aware of each other's feelings. The person whose foot got stepped on would put his or her arms around the partner. This would make the other person immediately feel more secure. Creating this plan strengthened Harry and Mollie's relationship. They now could count on each other to be there at times of insecurity.

Ways to Defuse Jealousy

In The Love of Your Life Workshops, we have discovered a number of ways to defuse the effects of jealousy. I want to share them with you here:

- Acknowledge and admit how you feel. This helps relieve the pressure.

- Make specific agreements about seeing other people. This one issue causes more problems than almost anything else. All you need to do is to agree to what actions you will take and not take.
- Don't break a trust. Broken trust is very difficult to repair in a relationship.
- Make sure your partner understands what's going on. In most cases, you can relieve your partner's anxiety by explaining the situation.
- Try to understand the threat. Often, jealousy occurs because of a misunderstanding on the part of one of the partners.
- Use jealousy as an occasion to stop and look at the relationship and the truth. You will be surprised at how enlightening this can be.
- Focus only on the threat. Don't try to use it as an occasion to correct your partner's other "faults."
- Do not make assumptions. The real situation often is not what you think it is.
- Negotiate with your partner. Often, you can work out an agreement that will help diffuse the situation as it occurs.
- Make sure you are on the same wave length as your partner. For instance, if your partner feels it's okay to date someone else and you don't, there is bound to be trouble.
- Renew each other's commitment periodically with your partner.
- Be patient and give it time.
- Give yourself some renewal, change your hairstyle, buy new clothes, lose weight.
- Nurture yourself. Give yourself lots of sympathy, then face the situation squarely.
- Stop judging yourself. Instead, discover the real problem and do something about it. For instance, if your jealousy is misplaced you need to work on that as a lesson. If your

partner is at fault, you need to decide what you actually need in this relationship and do something about it.

- Take time off. Sometimes when the jealous feelings become intense, it's better to take a short vacation from each other and try to think the problem through.
- Write out your feelings about it. Writing usually helps clarify the situation, and put it in perspective.
- Talk about it with a professional or a supportive friend.

Now, as an exercise, I want you to visualize a time you experienced jealousy. What happened? How did everyone react? How did it turn out?

Visualize the same scene a second time. This time, make it turn out the way you want it to so that you feel good about your reactions and can see the relationship grow as a result.

After you complete this exercise, answer these questions: What circumstances trigger jealousy in me? What circumstances trigger jealousy in my partner? Have any of my intimate relationships ended because of jealousy? How can I respond to prevent myself from becoming jealous? How do I communicate about jealousy with my partner? How can I handle jealousy in a more positive way?

Consider these answers carefully, decide which actions or reactions you would like to change, then begin to incorporate these changes in your life as you proceed through the remainder of this book.

Chapter Sixteen

The Intimate Process

Peace of mind comes from not wanting to change others.

—Gerald Jampolsky

[handwritten notes:]
Communication
willing to change: help ea.
other heal our wounds
(COMMITMENT)

[handwritten:] CHILDREN LOVER! and helper
of growth. I will not do
this alone!

[handwritten:] sense of Spirituality!

[handwritten:] 1888
MARS-VENUS.com
Big Sur Marathon.

Up to [...] rethinking
(and r[...] ial to good
relatio[...] s, putting
past r[...] munication,
trust, [...] ideal rela-
tionsh[...] n perspec-
tive, a[...] ons before
decidi[...] ly then do
you h[...] ship.

Lisa, for instance, explained to me that she had been in a relationship with a wonderful man for two years. They got along well and enjoyed many of the same activities such as skiing and dancing. The problem was that Lisa became panicky every time Bob talked to another woman. One afternoon while they were on the ski slopes, she spotted him coming up the ski lift laughing and talking to a pretty blond skier. When Bob got off at the top Lisa threw a fit, then headed down the mountain in a rage. When Bob finally caught up later, he told her that he couldn't take it anymore and that he thought it was time they stopped seeing each other. Lisa and Bob remained apart for almost four months before Lisa moved back in. The problem, however, remained unsolved. When Lisa came to my workshops, she began to understand and work through this unreasonable jealousy. By the time she was ready to go through the Intimate Process, discussed in this chapter, she was ready for a full, balanced relationship.

That is exactly where you also need to be at this point. If you haven't read the initial chapters carefully, go back and do this now. If you have done your Creating the Love of Your Life homework, but still feel you have problems, return to those chapters, and reread them before you start your Intimate Process.

Now, before you start making choices, I want to give you some instructions. First, the more you have paid attention to the initial chapters of this book, and the more you know what you want and need in a relationship, the closer you can come to actually obtaining it. Will you get everything? Of course not, but you can come very close.

Let me give you an example from one of my workshops. After finishing his Intimate Process, Brad, a thirty-year-old stockbroker, indicated that what he really wanted was a tall, statuesque blonde, who loved the outdoors, would take long wilderness hikes with him, enjoyed Shakespeare, came from a large family, and was Episcopalian. This seemed so specific that, in the beginning, I had doubts.

Within three weeks of attending my workshop, however, he showed up at my house one night with a beautiful blonde. They had just come from a weekend in the mountains. "She has," he told me smiling, "been quoting Shakespeare to me all weekend." The only place he missed was in the religious denomination. The woman was Methodist. But it didn't seem to make any difference.

After a number of years of conducting The Love of Your Life

Workshops, I can tell you, the process you are about to undergo really works.

The Guide

Now I want you (in writing) to start deciding what kind of person you really want to be with and what your relationship will look like. Up to this point, you probably haven't approached it like that. You've rationalized that you can't have everything you want. Every time you met someone, you did a lot of compromising. We all have done this. Often we just accept problem areas with a big sigh and try to make do. Sometimes this works, but if the gap between what we need, and what the other person provides is large, we set it up to fail. For a woman, for instance, a man might be a good dancer and a good conversationalist, but pay her very little attention. This may be okay in the beginning, but after a while it can become a sore point.

The first step in the Intimate Process is to take those needs, desires, and dreams out of your subconscious and bring them out where you can see what they really are. To do this, you must put it in writing and be as detailed as possible. Some of the questions and statements I am going to ask you to look over and select from may seem like nitpicking, but take each one seriously and answer it as carefully as possible. *The more you know of what you want the more you will end up getting.*

Besides including those traits or attributes you do want in an intimate partnership, include those things you do not want. When I started studying relationships, I created the first Intimate Process for myself. I had spent eight years making the same mistakes over and over, and I was discouraged. What I needed was a new way to make a good relationship happen. The first time I worked it out, I wrote down all the things I knew I wanted at that time. What I forget to do was to included what I didn't want.

Within four days, I met this man who was everything I

wanted. I don't have to tell you I was elated. But then I discovered he had a child, and I didn't want to become a stepmother. I loved children but my life was pointing in different directions at that time. I forgot to list it as an important point.

After two years and many problems created by the interference of the child's mother and by my failure to include this one very important point, we broke up. Needless to say, the next time I did the Intimate Process, I included those important things I didn't want, as well as those I did.

Let me give you another example. One of my clients wanted to create a relationship with a man who had money. However, he couldn't make this money just any way. It was okay, if he was a lawyer, a banker, an engineer, a business owner, or something similar. But Trish would be mortified if she had to tell her friends that the man in her life was a night watchman or bridge tollkeeper.

As you go along, I suggest your refer back to the learning process you went through in the earlier chapters. It helps to go over the sections where you described the characteristics that made your past relationships great or terrible. This is a process. What you want and need right now may change in the future. As you keep changing as an individual, so will your requirements. You can take out, add in, or change anything at anytime.

Now let's talk about the mechanics of the Intimate Process. Write in complete sentences and let the information flow off the top of your head. Writing in list form is not effective. Don't write in this book, but use separate sheets of paper and take as much time and as much space as you need. We are going to tap the real you, which means in effect tapping into your subconscious. What comes out might even surprise you.

Here's some examples of how you should cover each point:

Example: "I want a loving male partner who is considerate and caring and sensitive to my needs. I would also like him to be thoughtful and even tempered."

Example: "I would like her to be intelligent and to think through things before jumping to conclusions. I want her to defend her beliefs but also to leave me room to discuss the way I think."

Example: "My man will have a deep, steady, calm voice. Every time he speaks he radiates confidence. However, he certainly isn't conceited, and he will be very considerate of me."

It will help if you think of this process as creating a movie. You are the writer, the producer, the actor, the director, the audience, the critic, the scenery designer, the costume designer, the makeup artist, and the special-effects person. Use your visual imagination and actually see this person as you go along. If you are a man who would like a woman who doesn't use makeup, visualize a woman without makeup. Or if you prefer certain shades, and certain hairstyles, see these in your mind as you put this information on paper. If you are already in a relationship, just come from the deepest truth of what your ideal really is; don't write about the person you are with. Be as neutral and truthful as possible.

Take your time, but complete each section as you do it. You can, of course, fill it in briefly, then come back and work on it in greater detail later. But it works better if you just let the words flow once they start. Don't leave blank sections unless those characteristics are unimportant to you. Even then, it pays to include every detail.

Now, skim through the Intimate Process items to get the sense, then go back and describe in writing what you would like (in a partner) under each category. Some of these Intimate Process items are expressed in fragments to help trigger your thought process.

THE INTIMATE PROCESS
Relationship Types

Although many people today are looking for committed relationships or marriages, you can create any type of relationship that you want at this time. Choose from the following: friend, sexual, marriage, primary (monogamous), primary (with other partners), multiple lovers, group marriage. Do you want to live with your partner or maintain a separate residence?

Intimacy

General— How much time will he or she spend alone with you? Will you be a priority for this person? Will he or she be responsive, supportive, vulnerable, friendly, warm, caring, close, sharing, loving, open, tender, affectionate, touching, demonstrative in public and in private, have a sense of play and adventure, be flirtatious, and/or romantic?

Love

General— What love means to him or her? How does love make the other person feel? What role does love play in his or her life? How easily and how often does he or she fall in love? Is his or her heart open or closed? Does he or she find love pleasurable or painful? Can he or she accept love from others? Does he or she feel loved by you? And what is his or her capacity to love?

Social Skills

General— Sense of humor, fun, clever, witty, happy or sad? How much does he or she laugh? How much does the other person make you laugh? Is he or she moody, friendly and warm, arrogant and cold, interesting or boring? Does the other person have a sense of adventure? How flirtatious, mature or immature? How connected to his or her inner child? How predictable or unpredictable? Does he or she radiate friendship, or companionship? Is he or she flexible or rigid? How much attention does the other person need from you, or from others? Is he or she outgoing or shy?

Self-Esteem

General— Does the other person love himself or herself? Does the other person know who he or she is, feel powerful or powerless, and know how take care of himself or herself? Is the other person self-nurturing, able to say no, and committed to personal growth? Is he or she positive or negative? How does the other person face his or her imperfections? Does he or she spend time alone and have self-confidence? Is the other person strong or weak, joyful, secure or insecure, lonely or enjoys aloneness? Is that individual needy, have inner-strength, and self-acceptance? Is he or she independent or dependent?

Communication

General— How does he or she express himself or herself verbally, nonverbally and physically? How clearly and easily does the other person communicate? Consider the following: deceitful, open or secretive, confronts or avoids conflicts, asks for and gives support, and shares problems. Is he or she dramatic or dull, critical, and judgmental? Does the other individual listen to you, listen to themselves, and listen to others? He or she hears what is communicated, and is assertive. He or she is diplomatic, tactful, and sensitive. He or she is thoughtful or thoughtless, remembers special occasions, considerate or inconsiderate, respectful or disrespectful, takes others for granted, appreciative, aware of the needs of others and compassionate.

Creativity

General— Creative, imaginative, curious, awareness of abilities. How does he or she develop their creative talents? How does he or she use his or her creative abilities?

Clarity

General— Decisive or indecisive, make choices or takes what comes, clear or confused, focused, centered, knows where and how to look for answers. Pays attention, observes life, meditates and reflects.

Intellect

General— The other person is intellectual, scientific, technical, questions the meaning and issues of life and death. He or she has a high intellect and/or level of understanding. He or she defends his or her beliefs, is opinionated or open to the ideas of others. Other factors: education, knowledge, style— how the other person learns his or her lessons, how he or she uses his or her wisdom, how he or she seeks information, educational and cultural activities: lectures, classes, discussion groups, psychics, books, newspapers, magazines, television, radio, audio tapes, videos.

Spirituality

General— How spiritual, what part does spirituality play in life, how they grow spiritually, how intuitive, how he or she uses intuition, beliefs about religion, and reincarnation?

Sex

General— How important, how often, when, where, balance of giving and receiving pleasure, what it feels like, high or low sexual energy, passion, sensuality, kinky and eroding or routine, playful or serious, quiet or noisy, willingness to accept new ideas, who initiates sex? Sexual activity: seduction, foreplay, and afterplay. The communication before, during and after sex, orgasms, faithfulness, and the precautions taken.

Fears

General— What his or her fears are, how he or she handles fears, how much the other person worries, how fears hold him or her back, how he or she expresses and overcomes fears. Other considerations: defense mechanisms, courage, risk-taking, and phobias.

Emotions/Feelings

General— How do they acknowledge, express, and process anger, sadness, joy, resentment, guilt, shyness, depression, frustration, loss, anxiety, satisfaction, confusion.

Commitment

General— What commitments will he or she make to you and your relationship? How much does the other person want a relationship, how committed, how important is it? Willingness to make changes that will let the relationship work.

Other Qualities and Traits

General— Trust, struggles or strives, stays in control, manipulative, opportunistic, persistence, likes challenge, makes things happen or waits for things to happen, initiative, impulsive, spontaneous, fast or slow starter, peak performer or just gets by, resourcefulness, compassion, helper, giver or taker, judgmental or nonjudgmental, forgiving or unforgiving, prejudicial, loyal, has integrity, high or low energy, ambitious, lazy, optimistic or pessimistic, articulate, competitive, eccentric or conventional, possessive, stubborn or flexible, spiteful, calm, motivated, boastful, modest, spectator, violent, cynical, aloof, common sense, constructive or destructive, inhibited, tough, easy, pleasing, vicious, perfectionist or sloppy, hyper, envious, proud, tacky or tasteful, obstinate, cruel, teasing, cautious, competent, complacent, realist, dreamer, demanding.

Physical Description

Sex—male, female, heterosexual, homosexual, bisexual
Age—older, younger, same
Height—taller, shorter, same
Build—slim, stocky, muscular, heavy, average, broad
Hair—color, length, texture, thickness, curly, wavy or

straight, style, how much on body, arms, legs, chest, back, underarms, mustache, beard

Eyes—color, size, shape, expression, vision

Nose—size, shape

Mouth—size, shape, lips, breath

Teeth—real or false, hygiene, healthy

Hands—small or large, wide or slim, short or long, masculine or feminine

Fingernails—long or short, polished or bare, shape, manicured

Feet—large or small, shape, toe sizes, toenails

Breasts/chest—size, firmness, muscles

Buttocks—size, shape, firmness

Skin—color, texture, complexion

Attractiveness—handsome, beautiful, ordinary, more/same/less than you

Image—masculine, feminine, sophisticated, sexy, preppy, sleazy, artsy, cutsy, country, Wall Street, rocker

Origin—what country, what nationality

Voice—soft spoken or shreiky, talks too much or too little, pace, vocabulary, pronunciation, diction, use of harsh language, speaks clearly, mumbles

Self-awareness—vanity, ego, too much or too little attention paid to physical appearance

Clothing—stylish or out-of-date, color coordination, neat and clean or sloppy and dirty, variety, quality

Body—personal hygiene, how he or she smells, perspiration, posture, weight, how he or she walks, overall care

Health—healthy or sickly, high or low energy, diseases, allergies

Exercise—how much, what kind, agile or stiff

Home Environment

Location— Where, how close or far away from you, type of area

Description— House, apartment, condominium, room, owns or rents, lives alone or with others, spacious or cramped, modern decor or Salvation Army, artwork, plants, colors, coordination, view, neat or messy

Other— Permanent or temporary, how his or her home reflects their personality. How much importance is placed where he or she lives? How much time is spent there?

Work/Career

Fundamentals— Type of work, job or own business, stability, permanency, location, time schedule, coworkers, travel time, stress level, responsibilities, fulfillment, awareness of purpose or mission, goals, motivation, ambitions, hard working or lazy, fear of success or failure, commitment.

Money/Prosperity

Background-attitude— How much does he or she have, want to have? What earning potential, attitude of scarcity or abundance, practical or impractical, thrifty, frugal, wasteful, careless or careful, saver, investments, generous and giving or stingy and greedy, lives within means, lends money to others, buys on credit, and pays debts on time.

Family Background

General— How far away they live from you, large or small family, relationship with mother, father and other family members, closeness, conflicts, siblings, parents relationship with each other, still married or divorced?

Past Relationships

Present status— Single, separated, divorced, married, dating or not dating. Are they complete with past relationships? What are their present relationships like with ex-spouses and ex-lovers (too friendly, too distant)?
Past history— Was married or never married, how many times, lived with others, stormy or calm relationships.

Children

Status/relationships— How many, boys or girls, ages, what are they like, how much time does he or she spend with them, custody arrangements, when does he or she see them, where do the children live? How well does he or she get along with the children? How do they respond to you? How many does he or she want in the future?

Food

General— Eating habits, table manners, meal times, nutritional or junk foods, special needs, vegetarian, favorite foods, what is in their refrigerator, favorite restaurants, likes to cook or be cooked for, lives to eat or eats to live.

Habits

General— Smoker or nonsmoker, addictions, social drinking, nail biting, playing with hair, nose or ears, whistling, smiling, calm or nervous energy, homebody or always on the go.
Sleep— How much they need, sound or light, wakes up

happy or grumpy, day or night person, cuddles or sleeps apart?

Hobbies

Friends— How many, closeness, who are they, what they are like, how much time is spent with them? How do they react to you?

Interests— How important/How many things do you have in common: movies, theater, opera, ballet, reading, writing, dancing, parties, concerts, museums, gardening, sewing, knitting, massage, cards, collecting, travel, TV, music, chess, bingo, computers, skiing, swimming, boating, bowling, hunting, fishing, jogging, football, volleyball, baseball, hockey, basketball, golf, hiking, yoga, aerobics, ice skating, roller skating, ice hockey, polo, horseback riding, horse racing, car racing, hang gliding, bicycling, politics.

MANIFESTING THE RELATIONSHIP

Now that you have gone over the traits carefully, thought about them, and visualized your needs, you undoubtedly have a good idea of what you really want. The next step is to program your mind to make these needs a vital part of your personality. The techniques used are similar to self-hypnosis techniques used by psychologists to help people sleep, break bad habits, stop smoking, and more.

I have used them effectively over a number of years in my workshops. In practice, some people manifest their relationship almost immediately, others take much longer, but in the majority of cases it works. After one of my workshops, one young professional went to a party, realized that one of the men there, whom she had known for some time, was right for her, and started a committed relationship that lasted many years.

You now need to manifest the relationship you have described in the Intimate Process. Here are the steps I want you to take to reprogram this in your mind.

Step One: Get comfortable and relax and close your eyes. Take three deep breaths and relax deeply with each and every breath.

Step Two: Identify, or perceive, the part of your mind that is responsible for creating your relationships. How do you do this? You can do it in several ways. You can use a visual symbol that looks like you. This might be a little figure, a cartoon figure of you, your face filling your mind's eye, or anything else that you identify with.

Step Three: Acknowledge that aspect (that part of your mind) for doing everything you have told it to do in creating your relationships. Thank it for all you have learned from your relationships up to now, that your "mind" has provided you. Be sincere, appreciative, and come from love.

Example: I want to thank you for all of the relationships (the men or women) that you have created for me up to now. As a result of these past relationships, I have learned how valuable love and relationships are to me. Now I would like you to help me create this new relationship that will support who I am now and my purpose in life even more.

Step Four: Your subconscious (aspect) has done everything you have asked it to do so far. You are now giving it a new job. Ask your subconscious (aspect) to provide you with all the wants and needs that you have written down. Your subconscious (aspect) can read it directly from the pages you have just written. This will support what you want now. To reinforce this, it sometimes helps to read over (several times) your list of needs.

Step Five: Now thank that part of your mind that is going to do this new job. A simple thank you is enough.

Step Six: When you feel complete and satisfied, begin to come back. Once you have done this mentally, and are ready, open your eyes if they are closed.

You can do the Intimate Process in several ways. You can write this, say it in your mind, or say it out loud. I go to the beach and redo this every six months. I recommend the first few times that you do this process that you write it because it is so easy to become distracted and leave out important areas.

It also helps to visualize the person you are trying to "create."

You can do this by thinking what you want, by writing a statement about what you really want, or by telling other people about it. One of my clients does this with a device she calls her "God box." She writes what she wants on a slip of paper (for instance, it might say, "thank you God for giving me a new car") and drops it into her box.

Next, make yourself available by actively pursuing those interests you enjoy.

Now let the whole idea go. That is, resolve in your own mind that you are not going to push or search for what you have asked for, but you are going to let your subconscious mind create this. With your conscious desire just go about your business doing the things that make you comfortable.

You see this concept working in many other aspects of life. A couple tries for years to have a child. Then they give up and adopt a child, and within a month or two the wife becomes pregnant. I don't know how this works, but I have seen people desperately seeking a committed relationship with no results. Then, when they relax, let go of it and start to enjoy life, it can happen almost immediately.

Now, review the Intimate Process every six months.

Make the necessary revisions out of the changes you go through in that period of time. From now on, each relationship that comes into your life affirms what you want and what you do not want. Keep using that information.

In addition to my workshop participants, I have used this Intimate Process in my own life. I have already told you what happened the first time, when I forgot to manifest what I didn't want. Now let me tell you what happened when I found my husband Christophe. At the point I manifested this relationship I had a crazy life-style. I was by then a counselor who talked to people in crisis late at night, early in the morning, and on the phone while out of town. In addition, I was gone a lot. Most nights I was simply unavailable to fix dinner. In addition, I needed someone who was extremely supportive and wasn't bothered by jealousy. The reason for this was that many of my clients were good-looking men. Any partner of mine had to understand and not be affected by this. This was asking a lot.

But I went through the Intimate Process and developed the image I wanted, including those things I didn't want: children, a jealous partner, someone who expected me to maintain regular hours, and so forth. I met Christophe in one of my own workshops soon after I completed step #6 of the Intimate Process. At the time he was a chef at a San Francisco golf club. Later, I encouraged him to start his own business, collecting and selling autographs of famous people. This was something he had dreamed of doing for many years. He is so good at it, that he's become quite successful. He is also extremely supportive and gives me all the space I need. It has turned out to be a strong and wonderful relationship.

You can also use the Intimate Process to reprogram other issues that have become obstacles to creating an ideal relationship such as fear of intimacy, fear of rejection, jealousy, lack of self-confidence. Here's how that works.

One of my clients, Carol, lived in constant fear that no one would like her and that her ideas were worthless. She was thirty-five and had never been married.

In one of our sessions I asked her to make herself comfortable and relax. Next, I had her talk to the aspect of her mind that was responsible for creating her self-image and to picture this aspect in her mind's eye. She told herself that she was likable and thanked the image for making it happen. She also saw herself as having faith in herself and as having lots of friends and good committed relationships.

Within a few minutes she began to feel satisfied and good about herself. At this point I asked her to open her eyes and come back. She left smiling. I didn't hear from her for several days, then one day she called me to say the fear had disappeared. She had committed herself to the relationship with her boyfriend of ten months, and for the first time felt that he really cared. After that she seemed to gain confidence almost daily. The last time I saw her, she had just received a promotion at work and talked to me incessantly about her friends.

I sometimes also use this process to create short-range results. Recently, I was scheduled to go on a San Francisco radio call-in show to talk about The Love of Your Life Workshops. Waiting to go on I asked myself, "What do I really want to convey?" The answer was self-confidence. I then went through the process. I identified to myself that part of my mind that was responsible for self-confidence. I thanked it and asked that I become totally self-confident. I then went on the show and talked to a lot of callers. When I finished and came out of the studio, the station personnel in the outside room said, "Wow, did you sound confident . . . that was a great presentation!"

This is the process I use regularly in the workshops and believe me it works. The idea, of course, is to implant the image of the partner and the relationship you want in your mind. Then to develop those traits in yourself that will attract this individual. In my workshops I have both men and women create or attract their ideal relationship within hours, days, or weeks of manifesting their relationship. And what they have done you can do, too.

Now you are ready to begin SECTION III. In it we will discuss what you need to do to get ready for your ideal relationship and how to develop in yourself all of those qualities you are seeking in someone else. You will see what changes are necessary for you to make. Then we'll look at different ways of maintaining relationships with planned and unplanned romance. The last chapter will help you define your commitment to having THE LOVE OF YOUR LIFE.

SECTION III

SUCCEEDING

Chapter Seventeen

Making the Changes

We attract hearts by the qualities we display: we
retain them by the qualities we possess.
                    —Jean Baptiste Antoine Suard

After conducting The Love of Your Life Workshops for over eleven years, I have come to realize that if you are seeking certain qualities in someone else, you must develop them first in yourself.

Example: If you want a wealthy mate, but you are poor, you will not attract wealth. You need first to expand your wealth consciousness. This helps explain why people who think in terms of pinching pennies, often attract people who think in terms of pinching pennies.

Example: If you want a loving mate but have a lot of anger inside yourself, you will attract angry people. If you already feel loving toward people, you will attract that kind of person. It's up to you to develop those traits within yourself.

Example: If you are unhappy with life, you will attract people who are down on life. But, if you celebrate life, you will attract people who celebrate life.

* * *

Go through your list of wants and needs that describe your ideal relationship to see which of those qualities you already have that you want in a mate. The ones you do not have are those you need to develop within yourself.

You may find that: You want someone with a sense of humor, but discover that yours isn't very well developed ... You want someone who has inner peace, but you boil and fume, most of the time, inside ... Or you want someone who is stable, yet your life is unstable right now.

Your partner's traits can influence you to some degree. When Christophe came into my life, I was light, outgoing, and playful; he was very disciplined. I looked at my life before Christophe and asked how disciplined was I? I had to answer truthfully, "not very." I began to work on this over a period of time. Now, I can be very disciplined. After being with me for a number of years, Christophe is much more playful and outgoing than he was when we met.

Changes are Necessary

I find that if you do not have your ideal relationship, you are not operating at full capacity. You will grow alone, but with an ideal partner you will grow faster because more issues will surface to work on.

People are only truly happy when they are growing and making changes. Changes make you powerful and build self-love and self-worth. People who pursue their dreams often change their lives. I have discovered also that love often fades when one of the partners ceases to grow. Changes occur anyway, so why not make those changes that bring you what you want the most?

A Personal Inventory

I want you to take a type of personal inventory here by answering the following questions. They, combined with the Intimate Process in Chapter 16, will help you understand what you really want and need.

- How well do I know myself? Do I know what my goals are or how I feel about myself?
- How do I love and nurture myself? Some people never pamper themselves. They work all the time, or they spend their time doing things for others, not themselves.
- Am I happy with my appearance? My hair? My clothes? Posture? If not, you need to make some changes. Physical changes like these are much easier to make than changes in personal traits.
- What is my personality like? Am I interesting? Personable? Responsive? Happy? Outgoing? Fun? I'll explain how to tackle these changes later in this chapter.
- Would my ideal partner enjoy being in my home? Once you visualize your ideal partner from Chapter 16, you can answer this question easily.
- How satisfying is my work? Is my ideal mate compatible with what I am doing right now? Would changing jobs create the relationship I want? Again the answer to this question might point the way to needed changes.
- What talents and skills would I like to develop? This question can be answered after reviewing Chapter 16.
- Do I feel peaceful? Secure? Stable?
- What emotions, habits, and relationship issues need work? This question, too, should be answered with the help of Chapter 16.
- What are my lifetime goals? Think about this, then state them in clear and specific terms.

- What is my purpose in life?
- Is my life balanced by work and play?
- Why would I be an ideal relationship for someone else? This answer also helps pinpoint needed changes.

You may not be able to answer all of these questions. Others you will answer in the negative. All are designed to help you decide what changes you need to make. Read the overall list first from Chapter 16, then combine it with this. After that, make up a list of changes you would like to make in your life.

Fear of Making Changes

Some people make changes easily, others don't. The truth is that the fear of making changes keeps some people stuck and unfulfilled. Jack Canfield of Self-Esteem Seminars, says if you feel yourself resisting change use the slogan, "So what, do it anyway!"

One of my workshop participants, John, for instance, wanted to be more candid, and share more of himself with others. But each time he tried to be open in my workshops, he froze, couldn't say anything, and finally shut down.

"I'm the same way with my partner," he told me. "I wanted to tell her that I had been married and divorced, that I have a lifetime income and don't ever have to work again, and that now I'd really like to take the time to become an artist, but I can't. And not only can't I change enough to tell her, but actually making the changes terrifies me."

This may be an extreme case, but it's typical of how many people feel. Unfortunately, some people require a traumatic happening in their lives before they can make changes.

Some of the traumatic events that often trigger life changes are: A divorce . . . the loss of a job . . . going through a bankruptcy . . . the death of a partner, a son or daughter . . . a near-death experience . . . an accident . . . the loss of a friend . . . being sued . . . the end of a relationship . . . and more.

Louise, another client, was proud of her ability in the kitchen and was famous for her delicious Southern cooking. Just short of her fortieth birthday, Louise's husband asked for a divorce. For several months after it became final, she sat in her bedroom and felt sorry for herself. Then she decided she'd better get going. If she continued the way she was, she'd wind up old, bitter, and broke.

That's when she decided to go into business for herself. Since many people admired her Southern cooking, she decided to cater parties and group dinners using many of her famous recipes. The business became a success almost immediately. And within a year, she met and married a famous politician who attended one of her catered parties. "I needed to stand on my own two feet," she told me, "and create something of my own. But I wouldn't have done it without the divorce to spur me on."

Some of the changes people make after these experiences are: a career change, a new attitude on life, a change of image, a change in the way someone handles money, the creation of a new business, and similar adjustments.

Making the Changes

It's time now to really start making the changes. Here's what I suggest. Pick out those things you intended to change first. Then begin to use visualization on them. I recommend that you set aside ten minutes a day for each trait you intend to work on. During that time, see yourself establishing that trait.

For instance, maybe you want to work on honesty. See yourself going through a number of difficult situations and reacting honestly to each.

You accidentally dent someone's car in a parking lot, and

that person isn't there. See yourself getting out, writing a note to the car owner, and leaving it on the windshield.

See yourself at the end of a date. The other person says, "Will you call me?" Ordinarily you would say yes. But if you didn't want to call, you wouldn't. This time, you realize that you don't intend to call the person. See yourself telling them, "I had a good time, you're a wonderful person, but I need someone else. I think we should end our relationship right here." This is hard to do, but if you are working on this trait, keep at it, until it becomes second nature.

This same procedure can be used for any other trait you want to change.

As you begin to change, I want you to remember the following: It is never too late to change. Change can be easier than you thought. You are worth it.

I also want you to do the following. Be patient and gentle with yourself. Change a little at a time, do not try and do it all at once. Reach out to others for support. See yourself making positive steps every day. Become passionate and excited about making the needed changes.

Now, as we've done in every other chapter, I want you to ask yourself some questions: What am I pursuing instead of my relationship dreams? How am I making changes that will remove the obstacles and frustrations in my relationships? What is my biggest fear of change? How have I changed in the past year? Three years? Five years? Ten years? What is my commitment to having an ideal relationship? What is in the way of my having what I want?

Your Possessions

Possessions often represent the status quo. That is, possessions often represent the person we have become or are now, not the person we want to be. While changing possessions does not by itself help you make trait changes, it does represent a symbolic change, and helps create the mood you need.

Here is what I want you to do. Look around your home. Make a note of any items that represent standing still. Then get rid of anything that does not support your aliveness. Get rid of all items that have negative reminders of the past. And let go of anything that does not serve you anymore.

Clean out your closets, drawers, garage, basement, and attic.

Reorganize, rearrange, and move around your remaining possessions. This will move around and change old energy.

Let me give you an example. When we moved to a new house, I had a small expensive octagon-shaped table that was in perfect condition, but it simply didn't go with the new house or the energy level I was trying to create. It bothered me.

Without hesitating, I put it out on the street and attached a "Take Me" sign. Someone took it away in a few minutes. When I saw it go down the street, I felt relieved.

Color Adds Energy

I also suggest that when you change your possessions that you add energy to your surroundings by adding color. According to recent research conducted at the Wagner Institute for Color Research, the body reacts physically and chemically to all color.

Here are some of the emotional responses colors have been shown to produce: Red projects power, energy, intensity and daring . . . Yellow creates hopefulness and a cheerful spirit . . . Violet induces intimacy and relationships. Gentle colors project shyness and timidity. Blue creates a calming effect.

Add these colors with pictures, lamps, throw pillows, and other accessories.

Completing Past and Present Relationships

Along with making positive changes in your life, you also need to complete past relationships and clear them out of your present. Incomplete relationships drain energy. Energy scattered over nonfunctioning relationships also ties up the energy needed to make new connections.

By clearing negative energy and dead wood you make way for new higher level relationships to enter your life. Reread The Champagne Theory in Chapter 7.

Now let me give you an example of this. Jennifer, a forty-year old waitress and one of my clients, had a habit of breaking off relationships whenever she had a problem. Usually, she just "dropped" them, not even returning phone calls. Jennifer did this since she was seventeen. As a result she never achieved closure with any of them.

With Jerome, she agreed to trust thim, even if she saw him with another woman. One afternoon she spotted him with his secretary in a department store and blew up. Since then she has refused to talk to him. This issue needs to be resolved.

With Glen, she had promised to wait for him while he went overseas with his company for three months. Halfway through the time period, she moved in with another man. When Glen came home he was furious. This issue remains emotionally unresolved.

And with Jim, she wanted a committed relationship, he didn't. Yet, when he finally told her he could commit, she withdrew and went on to still another relationship. He's still trying to figure out what went wrong.

With Jennifer's energy scattered between three unresolved alliances, she is having trouble developing new and better relationships.

Now, take a look at all of your present relationships. Assess each one to see if it still belongs in your life. Compare these qualities with your needs from the Intimate Process list. Then if you need further clarity, evaluate them by listing the positive and negative qualities of each one.

A relationship is still incomplete if you have an emotional response to that person. It is complete when you feel neutral about that individual or have a flat response.

If there are any people on your list you feel angry at, write them letters expressing your anger as expressively as you can. Read these letters every day for two weeks and then tear them up. In some cases, you might want to communicate with them in person or on the telephone. You also might want to mail the letter. Choose the method that serves you best and the one which you feel will be most effective in helping to complete past unclosed relationships.

Buy a new address book and copy into it only the names of people who belong in your life now. Repeat this every six months. Using a Rolodex makes this process easier because you can just remove the old names. As you let go of the past you open the way for a new, brighter, more loving future.

Forgiveness

Forgiveness is sometimes part of completing and letting go of old relationships.

Forgive yourself as well as the other person, for you have both created whatever transpired between the two of you. Forgiveness will set you free, and create inner peace.

When you forgive someone else, you release any power of control that person may have over how you think, feel, or behave. By not forgiving, you freeze many of your feelings and attitudes in place. In my practice, I find that the inability to forgive is a major cause of suffering.

Here is a forgiveness process I want to suggest you go through.

1. Ask yourself: Am I willing to let go of the pain?

2. Remember and focus on what you love or loved about that person in the beginning.

3. Give to yourself whatever you need to forgive that other person. For instance, you might say, "I'll never forgive that person until he or she apologizes." Don't wait, apologize for yourself.

4. Ask if what you can't forgive in someone else could be the same thing that you do not love and accept within yourself.

5. Ask what lessons you now need to learn to forgive others.

6. Now, wish them well. Send them love. If they are out of your life, let them go. This often creates the power of forgiveness.

7. Breathe in white or yellow light and expand your boundaries. Imagine yourself becoming larger.

If you have a partner, periodically take a look and see if you need to forgive each other for anything. This will clear the air and make room for more lovingness between you.

The more you practice forgiveness, the easier it becomes.

Broken Agreements

All agreements need to be completed. When you do not keep your word, you lose trust in yourself and the trust of the person you made the agreement with. When I was a member of a support group, we had only two rules: you had to give twenty-four hours' notice if you were going to be absent and not be late. If you did break an agreement, you had to bring a special snack for the group next time as a way of restoring the broken trust.

I recently gave a party for my husband and invited a number of people. I ordered food for those who indicated they would be there. Twelve people who said they would show up, didn't. As a result, I threw away a tremendous amount of food. While this particular broken agreement isn't all that important, many are.

Remember Jennifer? She had promised to wait for Glen while he went overseas with his company for three months. But she didn't do it. This is the type of broken agreement that must be cleared up before an individual can move on with a clear conscience. Jennifer has broken a trust, and desperately needs to reestablish trust in herself before she can grow again and move forward.

What she needs to do first is to talk it over with Glen, explain the problem as best she can, apologize, and ask forgiveness. After that she needs to work on trust as described earlier in this chapter.

Of course, even if you make an agreement, you can negotiate any change you want. But you must always complete old agreements before you can move on with full energy and purpose.

Making changes is not always easy. But it is necessary if you are to prepare yourself to attract the relationship you really want. If you are really serious about Creating The Love Of Your Life, you will find this chapter to be one of the most important in the book, for it offers you the keys to a wonderful future.

Chapter Eighteen

Romance

Relationships are adventures in romance and creativity.

—Susan Scott

Even though many people view romance as "a love affair," romance is not about sex.

Romance is an attitude. It is another way of communicating to someone else that they are special to you.

Romance is not what you do, or how you communicate another's specialness. It is more how you feel when you are doing it. Romance also means doing something that shows the other person how you feel.

George, an acquaintance of mine, decided to help keep a spirit of adventure in his relationship with his fiancée, Marge, by treating her to an unexpected romantic escapade every few months. One Friday night, he picked her up from work in downtown Sacramento, California, and told her he was taking her for a night on the town. She didn't pay much attention to where they were going until he pulled up at the airport. It turned out her night on the town was to be in Los Angeles, four hundred miles and an hour away by air. They flew to Los Angeles and had dinner in a restaurant overlooking the water. In the middle of the meal, a violinist (hired by George) appeared to serenade Marge. They then caught the last plane back at the end of the evening.

That, of course, was an elaborate romantic evening. It doesn't have to be that complicated. The next weekend, Marge served a candlelight dinner for George on the balcony of her apartment. The candlelight and the lights of the city made it quite romantic.

Being romantic requires imagination, creativity, originality, inventiveness, and improvisation skills. To see what you need, conjure up a vision of what you want romance to look and feel like.

For instance, romance may mean doing something unusual with your partner every weekend, it may mean you want your partner to bring you gifts now and then, or it may mean you want a partner that will read books out loud to you.

Stop now and decide what romance means to you. Then create some pictures in your mind of romantic moments. You might, for instance, conjure up a picture of yourself in a taxi going to the opening night of the opera. It might be a mental picture of you and your partner riding through a park in a horse-drawn carriage. Or it might be a picture of you and a partner standing by a window looking down at the twinkling city lights.

Romance is magnetic. When you do something romantic for someone else, they are often inspired to do something romantic back. It is a catalytic process. When you let someone enter the freeway in front of you, they often wave thanks, and then feel more inclined to return the gesture to someone else.

Romantic attitudes lead you toward new journeys and new adventures, because the feelings created by romance help change old routines.

A romantic attitude often has nothing to do with how much you spend, because I know people who always have a romantic time eating at McDonald's.

One of my clients took her boyfriend to a fast-food restaurant, spread a tablecloth over the table, pulled out a candelabra from her purse, put it on the table, and then read poetry to her boyfriend for the next half hour. She created quite a stir, but he loved it.

In another example, married clients John and Maggie loved each other, but they never went anywhere and never did anything. This went on for years. John worked two jobs to save to buy a home of their own, so they seldom saw each other, except on Sundays. This put a strain on the marriage.

John, however, decided to do something about the problem. One Sunday morning, he served Maggie strawberry waffles on a tray in bed. The next Sunday, he talked her into seeing the sunrise from the roof of their apartment building; the Sunday after that, he came in with a huge bouquet of flowers. From then on they did something different every weekend. Each one was a small thing, but taken all together, they helped put some of the excitement back in their relationship.

One time, when Christophe and I were out of town for a weekend, my husband asked the woman at the front desk at our hotel which restaurant was the most romantic. She replied, "I take my romance with me!"

The Importance of Romance

Often, after a couple has been together for a while, they settle into a routine. Unfortunately, while routines smooth daily living, they also create predictability and boredom. In time, boredom can lead to the breakup of the relationship itself.

I have found that it takes more than just love to make a relationship last. Plants require sunlight, food, and water to continue to flourish. In the same way, relationships must be nurtured with romance. Romance provides much of the attention that mates need from each other and helps keep a relationship alive and growing. In addition, it often helps a couple to fall in love all over again.

Benefits of Romance

Romance provides many benefits to a relationship. I want to go over them for you now to make the point.

- Romance allows you to give pleasure and to receive it from someone special.
- It shows how you feel toward another person. Actions speak louder than words.
- It overrides the fear of risking.
- It always compliments the receiver. What individual doesn't feel good when someone else makes a romantic gesture toward them? Even the simple act of gift giving can make someone feel good all over.
- Romance keeps you in the moment.
- Romance builds traditions. Each year, on the anniversary of our first date together, my husband and I return to the same restaurant and have dinner at the same table.
- Romance builds intimacy. It always helps create a tie between two people.
- It builds memories. You can always recall those romantic times in your past. It's the other times you often can't remember.
- It is fun! Remember how good you felt when you danced the night away with someone special . . . when you stood at the top of a hill with someone you cared about . . . when a special person unexpectedly showed up and surprised you. You add some others.

The Two Phases of Romance

There is, of course, a difference between being romantic, romance, and a romance. We often think of a romance as the courting phase of a relationship. There are generally two phases. The first phase establishes the relationship.

This includes: seduction, the chase, the challenge of capture, winning, and tempting. I find this to be the easiest part in any relationship.

The second phase is maintaining the relationship. This includes finding ways to keep it alive and growing, as well as enhancing it. This is the most challenging phase of any romance. This is what we've been talking about when we say that a relationship must be kept alive by being romantic.

Romantic Ideas

I'd like to offer a few suggestions to help you include romance in your present and future relationships.

Romance can be planned or unplanned.

Planned romance requires that you make the arrangements ahead of time. This might mean making reservations at a restaurant, arranging a surprise party, packing for a trip, and more.

Planned romance has some advantages.

• The time for romance has already been set aside. Often couples complain that they get so busy that they don't have the time to do special things together. Planning allows you to set aside a certain time each week, or to simply schedule time for a special event such as a picnic, or an afternoon making love.

• It helps organize a busy life. Again when time is a problem, planned romance provides the solution. Many two-income couples find this to be a tremendous advantage.

• There is more time to make preparations. For instance, if you plan a romantic dinner for your mate, you have time to shop for what you want, find just the right candles, and so forth. This helps add to the atmosphere.

• Planning increases the anticipation for you and usually your partner. For example, if you intend to go away together for a romantic weekend, the anticipation always builds as the weekend draws near.

Planned romance has some disadvantages.

• It can bring expectations. And unfortunately, it's almost impossible to live up to them all. For instance, what if it rains on that romantic weekend, or it takes longer to get there than you expected? Everyone needs to anticipate letdowns and to allow for them.

• It lacks spontaneity. Sometimes you can surprise a partner with planned romance, but generally it lacks the element of surprise or the adventure that comes from doing something on the spur of the moment.

• You might be in the mood to have a different experience at that time. For that romantic weekend, for example, you planned to go to a local resort, but when the weekend actually arrived, you were really in the mood to go to the seashore.

Unplanned romance is making something romantic and special out of what is happening at the moment. Unplanned romance might include taking off your shoes and wading in a pond, buying flowers on impulse at a street-side flower stand, or picking up a gift at the last moment to surprise your partner.

Unplanned romance has some advantages.

- It always has the element of adventure and surprise.
- It needn't be elaborate.
- It keeps your partner guessing.

Unplanned romance has some disadvantages.

- It can upset the routine. Sometimes it's fun to wind up at a park concert when you intend to spend the day shopping. But it can be unsettling if surprises like this occur all the time.
- It can seem trivial unless you throw in other, more elaborate planned romantic events from time to time.

Now, I'd like to give you some suggestions that will help put romantic adventure back in your relationship. You can: Celebrate a birthday on the wrong day . . . Bake or cook a surprise treat . . . Take dance lessons . . . Practice dancing with your mate . . . Take turns reading romantic books out loud . . . Share an ice cream soda with two straws that are tied together . . . Get up to see the sunrise with your mate . . . Walk instead of driving . . . Work a crossword puzzle together . . . Make a collage of some of the activities you do together . . . Go picnicking in an unusual spot . . . Try a new place for an adventure . . . Plan an outing without telling your partner where you are going . . . Perform for your partner: play an instrument, dance, sing . . . Leave unexpected messages on the answering machine . . . Dress your partner instead of undressing them . . . Set aside special days of giving, receiving, silence, laughing, joke telling, rhyming, creating projects.

Let me share with you what one of my workshop participants does. Tom, a salesman at Macy's Monterey, has been happily married for sixteen years. He and his wife celebrate their anniversary on the twenty-first of every month plus a half-versary in February. They always go out to dinner on that day, and it is Tom's job to remember to make the plans each month. For that occasion, he also always brings his wife a special gift. One month he might buy candy, another time he'll pick up some fancy stationery.

For this occasion, they dress up and Tom buys Maggie a corsage. While this is planned romance, it helps keep their marriage alive. "I always look forward to these occasions," Maggie told me. "Tom has such a twinkle in his eye. I love it."

If you are part of a couple at this time, I suggest that you get in the habit of always having something scheduled in your appointment calendars to look forward to. A little anticipation can go a long way. It feels good to have something special coming up to think about.

Now, let me give you a reality check. Ask yourself: In what ways am I romantic? What are some romantic adventures I would like to share with my partner? What stopped us from having these adventures? What was my most romantic date?

Think about these for a while, then use them and the other information in this chapter to help put the romance back in you and your partner's life.

Chapter Nineteen

Commitment

*Commit yourself to a dream. Nobody who tries to
do something great but fails is a total failure.
Why? Because he can always rest assured that he
succeeded in life's most important battle—he de-
feated the fear of trying.*

—Robert H. Schuller

Committed relationships are the goal of most couples in the '90s.
Commitments, of course, vary from couple to couple. One couple
may see commitment as a long-term relationship. Another may
see commitment as a dedication to one another, still another
may see commitment as an engagement or a marriage.

Without commitment, it is impossible to derive the full benefit of any long-term relationship.

When you make a commitment in a relationship, such as
becoming engaged or getting married, all of your unresolved
issues will tend to surface. Some of the unresolved issues can be
about abandonment, about your mother or father, or broken
agreements.

Marriage is considered to be the highest level of commitment in a relationship. Nothing changes with your unresolved
issues because the form of your relationship has changed. You
have to take responsibility and work through those issues in
order to resolve them.

In the workshops, when we reach the section on commitment, I usually hear silence or loud moans (mostly from the

single attendees). All of a sudden, breathing becomes difficult for many of the participants. They react as though commitment is the worst thing they can think of.

I've seen this reaction in every workshop for over eleven years now, and it still surprises me. Up to this point, everyone who participates is intent on creating their ideal relationship. When it comes time to consider committing to that relationship, however, the whole mood changes.

The problem is not with the issue of commitment, but in misunderstanding the meaning of commitment. Once it is understood, the fear of commitment dissolves and the relationship continues with a new perspective.

Lack of Commitment

Commitment is scary to some people because it implies that something will stay the same, and that it will be forever.

One of my clients, Doris, lived with Jordan for almost a year. During that time, she told herself that they were just trying out the relationship.

One weekend Jordan asked her to marry him. Suddenly, all her past relationships flashed before her eyes: the bitter arguments with her former husband, the boyfriend who stole money from her, the unhappiness she found in her last relationship. Doris just sat there shaking, unable to say anything. Finally, she crawled into bed and spent that afternoon sleeping. The next day she moved out of the apartment. After her past relationship experiences, she still couldn't commit.

I find that many of the people I see fear commitment because they dread the pain of past relationships, or they simply don't want to give up the freedom they now have.

When there is a lack of commitment, there might be a lack of trust. Running from commitment is running from love. When someone will not make a commitment, they could be afraid of a number of things.

Here are some common fears of commitment:

- Being controlled.
- Being trapped.
- Loss of self.
- Loss of independence and freedom.
- Fear that their boundaries will dissolve.
- Having self-doubt.
- Doing things out of duty instead of wanting to.

Ann, a client of mine, is forty-two and has never made a commitment in a relationship. She always shows up for work, never misses her appointments, and generally seems pleasant and responsible. When I asked her about her fear of commitment, it was complex. "I always have to leave a way out for myself. I can't fully commit to even simple day-to-day things, even meeting someone for coffee." When I probed a little further, Ann admitted that, "I always fear there is commitment on one side only and not on the other side. I need assurance about the commitment from the other side first."

Ann's lack of commitment occurs only in personal, intimate relationships. She said, "I can't commit if it feels like life or death. I don't commit because I don't expect the other person to reciprocate. Maybe I don't know what a real commitment is."

Ann believed if she was truly committed she would feel relaxed, clear, and confident. Commitment will not bring relaxation, clarity, or confidence to you unless you already possess those qualities and bring them with you to the relationship. A commitment can never be made with more energy than a person believes in himself. No commitment to another person can be stronger than a commitment to yourself.

If you have high self-esteem and self-confidence, if you have developed a strong ability to trust, and you have great communication skills and your lack of commitment is still present, there is a strong possibility that you are trying to commit to the wrong person.

A lack of commitment can arise when intuitively you feel something is not right. Check out what your intuition says.

A lack of commitment can keep the relationship based on rejections of each other's weaknesses.

A real commitment exists only if it comes from your heart. You cannot make a commitment because you have to. It is only real when it is felt deeply, when you really want it. A couple I once knew, Vallerie and Tony, had been living together for two years. Vallerie was at the end of her rope because she was ready to get married but Tony had no inclinations in that direction. After many stressful arguments, Tony finally gave in because he knew he would lose Vallerie if he didn't commit to marriage. A divorce resulted only three months later.

Some see making a commitment as a last-ditch effort to make a relationship work. If the commitment is implemented out of fear rather than from love, it can easily be ill-fated. If the commitment you have feels forced, or is an attempt to please your partner, it is likely that it is the wrong commitment for you.

When two people have different levels of commitment, they are not in the same relationship. If your partner tells you, "I'm committed," but then he or she doesn't back it up with their actions, it is time to reevaluate and redefine each other's commitment.

Making Positive Commitments

When a commitment is made to the right person, many positive feelings ensue. Many clients over the years have expressed that commitment feels natural and destined, like it is in the best interest for each of you, like the beginning of healthier and more loving times, like something to be proud to be part of, a source of meaning and direction, a sense of wholeness and completeness, empowering, very fortunate, exciting, and a sense of congruency.

Here are some other positive aspects of commitment:

- Deeper sharing.
- Stronger sense of stability.
- Trust.
- Mutual support.
- Greater synergy.
- Fun.
- Love.
- Well-defined and firmer boundaries.
- Autonomy.
- Expanded creativity.
- More productivity.
- Secure communication.
- Reinforcement of your goals.
- More clarity and purpose.
- More focused energy and attention.
- More focus on the present and future rather than the past.
- Problem-solving.
- More tendency to accept each other as you are rather than what you are not.
- Belief that together you form something greater than your individual selves.
- Deeper lessons.
- More investment for the relationship to be the best it can be.

Strengthening Commitment

Here are some ways to strengthen your relationship commitment:

1. Focus on what you will get from commitment rather than what you would lose.

2. Reaffirm your beliefs in yourself, your partner, and your relationship.

3. See your commitment as part of your larger goals.

4. Review your commitments that worked in the past and remember what made them work and what you learned from them.

5. Try to understand any deeper feelings you have been avoiding.

6. Take one step at a time. Don't try to work on too many issues at once or you will scatter your energy.

7. Define your relationship goals AGAIN.

8. Go as slow or fast a pace that is comfortable.

9. Plan and work together.

10. Develop an attitude of giving more.

11. Communicate, communicate, communicate.

Defining Your Commitment

Your commitment to a relationship defines what the relationship is, and how things are between the two of you. Commitment is an agreement to take responsibility to make the relationship work. It is an agreement, it is not a contract. Agreements can be changed. Not only is commitment necessary for the relationship to work, but also for the relationship to grow.

Two of my clients, Barbara and Hank, went together for almost two years. During that time, they enjoyed each other, and shared many common interests. But as Hank said, "We never grew really close." At the end of the two years, Hank asked Barbara to commit to him to the exclusion of other partners. She refused.

After that, the relationship was never quite the same. And after a series of arguments, the couple broke up.

"I am the sum of my commitments or in other words, I am what I chose to stand up and be counted for, and those choices define me." Martin Buber.

Of course, commitment doesn't mean just one thing. Some couples commit to each other only tentatively, others create a very deep and lasting commitment. In addition, I find that as a relationship grows, so does the commitment.

When clients complain that they received only a tentative commitment from their partners, I tell them to relax. If it is a problem within the relationship itself, they must communicate needs. If the relationship is not right or appropriate for them, they should consider creating a new relationship.

The main thing I feel is to first make a commitment, no matter how small. I always suggest that couples talk about each other's commitment so that they will know where each partner is in the relationship. Your level of commitment indicates how much time and energy you are willing to give to the relationship.

George, a technical writer for a Silicon Valley computer firm, was literally dedicated to his work. He spent at least ten hours a day, six days a week working on his projects. George spent the remaining time sailing on a nearby lake.

Because of these outside interests, George realized that his commitment to his fiancée Alice was lukewarm, at best. Many weekends he spent by himself. When she complained, he had to admit that the relationship came in dead last. The result was that Alice gave him back his ring, and he immersed himself in his job and boat. Some day George will be ready for a committed relationship, but now isn't that time.

Warren, on the other hand, realized that although he loved his job, that Cindy was really his life. He was devoted to her and would do anything to make her happy. If you were to rate George's level of commitment on a scale of 0 to 10, George would rate a 3 or 4. Warren's commitment could be rated at an 8 or 9.

I also want to stress that commitments change and grow just as the partners change and grow. You can change your commitment as you change your life. But to make a relationship work, you must know how much energy you intend to put in it, and renew it frequently.

Now, ask yourself: Are you in a committed relationship right now? If not, are you afraid of commitment? Why? Do you feel commitment will result in pain? Or loss of freedom? If you are in a committed relationship how would you rate your commitment on a scale from 0 to 10? If your commitment level is low, why? Are you willing to work on your commitment and your relationship and see both grow? What are you willing to do? If not, why not?

The answers to these questions will let you see exactly how you feel about commitment right now. Understand that it is impossible to have a long-term growing relationship without commitment. If you seek a good relationship, yet fear commitment, you will need to work on this issue just as you did for the other issues in Chapter 17.

As I have seen many times in my workshops, the process works. At this point, you will have a better understanding of yourself than you did before you read this book . . . You will have a new perspective on your past, present, and future relationships . . . You will understand which lessons you still need to learn . . . And you will know exactly the kind of relationship you want and need.

You are now well on your way to Creating the Love of Your Life.

Dear Reader;

Susan Scott is available for speeches and workshops.

If you would like to schedule a workshop or lecture in your town, or if you are interested in tapes, workshop topics and schedules, or phone consultations, please write:

Susan Scott
P.O. Box 51937
Pacific Grove, CA 93950-6937